Girl with Glasses

Girl with Glasses

MY OPTIC HISTORY

Marissa Walsh

SIMON SPOTLIGHT ENTERTAINMENT
New York • London • Toronto • Sydney

Some names have been changed.

There is no harm whatsoever in reading in dim light.
—ROBERT CYKIERT, OPHTHALMOLOGIST,
IN *Real Simple* MAGAZINE

SIMON SPOTLIGHT ENTERTAINMENT
An imprint of Simon & Schuster
1230 Avenue of the Americas, New York, New York 10020
Text copyright © 2006 by Marissa Walsh
Illustrations copyright © 2006 by Jason Logan
SIMON SPOTLIGHT ENTERTAINMENT and related logo are trademarks of
Simon & Schuster, Inc.
Designed by Steve Kennedy
Manufactured in the United States of America
First Edition 10 9 8 7 6 5 4 3 2 1
Library of Congress Cataloging-in-Publication Data
Walsh, Marissa, 1972–
Girl with glasses : my optic history / Marissa Walsh. —1st ed.
p. cm.
ISBN-13: 978-1-4169-2493-7
ISBN-10: 1-4169-2493-0
[1. Walsh, Marissa. 1972– 2. Myopia—Patients—Biography. 3. Eyeglasses.
4. Myopia—Humor.] I. Title.
RE938.W35 2006
362.197'7550092—dc22
[B]
2006019862

For Matt

Contents

Glasses worn by a woman in the cinema do not generally signify a deficiency in seeing but an active looking, or even simply the fact of seeing as opposed to being seen.

—*Femmes Fatales*, MARY ANN DOANE

We don't see things as they are. We see them as we are.

—ANAÏS NIN

Four Eyes Are

Better than Two

Until our century, a respectable woman kept her eyes modestly averted.

—*Sexual Personae,* CAMILLE PAGLIA

My optic history has included ten pairs of prescription glasses, one pair of prescription sunglasses, and countless pairs of contact lenses. Since third grade, when I got my first pair of glasses, I have been photographed with and without glasses. I have worn my contacts so religiously that no one knew I wore glasses. I have worn my glasses so religiously that no one knew what my face looked like without them. I have been to contacts and back again. And the blinder I've gotten, the clearer I've been able to see.

Although I didn't officially begin wearing glasses until age eight, I was born a Girl with Glasses (GWG). But it wasn't until college, surrounded by a gang of cool glasses-wearing girls, that I was able to fully embrace my four-eyed fate. Glasses became more than just an accessory; they became part of my personality, my identity—part of me.

As a teenager, I didn't have Tina Fey, Lisa Loeb, and

Janeane Garofalo to emulate. No Frances McDormand wearing glasses to the Oscars. No Lane on *Gilmore Girls* playing drums in her band. When I first started wearing glasses, there weren't exactly options. You had bad eyes, you wore glasses. There was no LASIK surgery. There were no soft contacts. Disposables? Colored? Please. The only option was hard contacts. With the emphasis on "hard." Now being bespectacled is a conscious decision, because everyone knows you don't have to wear them. It's a choice. A choice about how you want to view the world and, more important, how you want the world to view you.

Girls with Glasses are observers; our interaction with the world is often from a distance, from behind the protection that our glasses afford us. Growing up behind glass, one often forgets that people can see in, too.

Marissa Walsh

I'm going to take you somewhere. It's time you began to see the world. You're eleven years old and it's time you saw something.

—OLE GOLLY TO HARRIET, *Harriet the Spy,*
LOUISE FITZHUGH

CAROL BRADY: *"Jan, I think you may need glasses."*
JAN BRADY: *"Glasses! Oh no, Mom! Not glasses! They'll make me look absolutely positively goofy!"*

—The Brady Bunch

The First Pair

1980~1984

Wait and See

The first test I ever failed was a vision test. It was third grade, and the people who came to school every year to test our eyes and ears showed up with that portable machine with the View-Master binocularlike window, except that instead of picture slides inside, there were letters. Which I couldn't read.

Before the eye and ear people came, I thought maybe it was my teacher's fault. Mrs. Babin liked to write math problems on the blackboard for us to copy down. One day I couldn't read the numbers on the board anymore. At first I chalked it up to the glare from the sun coming in the window. There was also the fact that I hated math; it was my worst subject. But the problem recurred—even on rainy days. I didn't know what was wrong. But I ignored it, thinking eventually my vision would return to normal. It didn't.

I had spent many hours at my grandparents' house sitting in their dark living room, reading. When Nana and Papa saw me, they would always switch on the light and say, "Don't read in the dark; you'll hurt your eyes."

I hadn't listened.

When Mrs. Babin gave me a note to take home to my parents, I knew exactly what it was for. The jig was up. I was tempted to "forget" to give them the bad news, but like most GWGs, I was too good a girl. And nervous about my math grade.

As a baby I had been diagnosed with asthma, but that condition had set in too early for me to remember life before it. It and its limitations had always just been a part of me. Glasses had not, and I didn't want them to be. The only person who wore glasses in my family was Nana Walsh, and she was old. Very old. How could I need glasses? I was just a kid.

The only two kids I knew who had glasses were my younger cousin Eric, and one of the many girls in my class named Michele, who was cross-eyed. I did not identify with either of them.

Private Eye

I was not alone in my newfound nearsightedness. My brother Steven, fifteen months my junior, joined me in the four-eyed ranks around the same time. Steven was never one to let me have my own thing for very long. I don't remember what kind of glasses he got—I don't even remember how his revelation came about. I've obviously blocked it out. He wears contacts now.

My parents were confused. They didn't wear glasses; their siblings didn't wear glasses; my other brother, Joseph, didn't wear glasses. Where had this glasses-wearing gene come from? They were also probably embarrassed that, like the inevitable head lice, it had been discovered not at home or at our pediatrician's office, but at school.

The Purchase

Failing the vision test meant that I had to get glasses. And as a soon-to-be girl with glasses in Lynn, Massachusetts, it meant that my mother brought me to the aptly named Mr. Specs on the corner of Western and Chestnut. Mr. Specs was on the same block as the toy-slash-craft store where I bought my latch-hook rug-and-potholder-making kits.

Mr. Specs was a bespectacled gentleman (just a face, actually) in a top hat—sort of a cross between Mr. Peanut and Mr. Tux. I'm not sure how old Mr. Specs was; he seemed ageless, like he had always been there, waiting.

Sadly, Mr. Specs had only one small children's section. (I was a discriminating shopper.) Regardless, I embraced the ritual of picking out frames. Every Girl with Glasses knows this is the best part. I am sure I tried on every pair of acceptable girls' frames they had, and examined myself in the mirror while asking my mother's opinion, before choosing beautiful round plastic frames in my favorite color, purple. The purple was subtle—almost lavender, really. My first pair came with a bright red case to keep them safe.

I loved them.

At First Sight

At the Tony Awards a few years ago, Nicole Kidman walked to the podium to present an award, put on a pair of glasses, and said, "I need these, *unfortunately.*" (The emphasis is mine.) I was as shocked as anyone when Nic pulled out those specs. How far away was the teleprompter she was trying to read? If she needed glasses for distances, did that mean that the rest of the evening (sans glasses) she couldn't see? Had she waved to Nathan Lane thinking he was Hugh Jackman? And, really, isn't that the definition of celebrity? We can see them but they can't see us.

I, too, was a Part-Time Girl. At first. Why ruin my red-carpet look when I only needed glasses for two minutes a day to read my own teleprompter, the blackboard?

I dutifully carried my little red case to and from school every day in my bag with my lunch. When I got to school, I put the case in my desk, and put my glasses on only when

I needed to read the board. I never wore them otherwise. I was never photographed in them. The only people who knew of their existence were my fellow third, fourth, and fifth grade classmates. (And some of them probably hadn't even noticed.) Seeing was good, but I wasn't ready to have my appearance defined by my glasses. They were not a part of me. Even if they *were* purple.

Eye for an Eye

My best friend at the time was a girl named Cindy. Her real name was Cynthia with a *y*, and I always wondered why we didn't call her Cyndi instead of Cindy. She was the one who had the sleepovers where we did séances and tried to levitate the slightly plump Tracey. She was the one the boys liked. Not coincidentally, she was also a Pop Warner football cheerleader. The *head* cheerleader. The captain. During recess, Cindy taught us—the noncheerleaders—cheers, and we followed along, clapping and shouting in unison ("BE AGGRESSIVE! B-E AGGRESSIVE!"). We didn't cheer for anyone or anything in particular.

My parents would not let my brothers play football or hockey. ("Too violent!") And they would not let me be a cheerleader, probably for the same reason. They didn't care that I already knew all the cheers, that I'd be a shoo-in at tryouts, that I was losing my best friend because I wasn't involved in the thing that was most important to her. Cindy and I used to scheme about how I could try out without my parents knowing. But I never did. And maybe deep down I knew that being a cheerleader might not be the right fit for me. But oh, how I longed for that color-coordinated outfit! The snug sweater! The short pleated skirt! The pom-poms! The saddle shoes!

Michele with one *l*, a full-time glasses-wearer, did try out. Now recess featured *two* real cheerleaders. And the rest of us. Before long Michele started looking at me sideways, and I began trying to get Cindy to say that I was her best friend. I've since learned that if you need to make someone tell you that she is your best friend, she definitely isn't.

Eyes Without a Face

Things changed around the sixth grade. This is when it usually happens. Some girls are wearing training bras, and you are not. Some girls are dating, and you are not. Some girls are cheerleaders. I was not.

During sixth grade, out of necessity, I began wearing my glasses for more than just reading the board. I became a Full-Time Girl. I made the decision one day at soccer practice. My friend Chrissie and I had been dropped off early and were hanging out at the field waiting for the rest of the team to arrive, when I heard two girls yelling my name. Some shapes in the distance waved and shouted hello. I waved back but had no idea who they were. It drove me nuts, like receiving an unsigned valentine. More important, it proved that my eyesight was getting worse.

It was easier to just keep them on all day, since I now seemed to need them all day, except to read. Leaving them on my nose was preferable to wearing them on a chain around my neck, like my grandmother did when she waitressed, or on top of my head, which is where one of my aunts often forgot she had left hers.

Plus, I had braces.

Uncle.

Vision Quest

My glasses did not keep me from waging a spirited campaign to become sixth-grade class president. I set out to ask each member of my class to vote for me. I made lists and checked off who had made verbal commitments. I made buttons and little strips of paper to leave on people's desks. I plastered the hallways with campaign posters featuring hot-air-balloon stickers and clever slogans like "Aim High!" I asked an artistic girl I was barely friends with to make bookmarks with which I bribed girls: "You can have one, but only if you vote for me." I was *Election*'s Tracy Flick, without the cupcakes.

I won, but only by one vote.

My glasses didn't keep me from entering the citywide sixth-grade speech contest, either. As an Irish-Catholic Massachusetts Democrat, I naturally chose JFK's inaugural address, and was selected as one of my school's two participants. The other delegate from my school was a girl named Melissa, who recited Martin Luther King Jr.'s "I have a dream" speech. Cindy was an alternate with the Gettysburg Address, a popular choice.

Flush from winning the election, I decided I wanted to win the speech contest too. I asked my father what I had to do to win; he told me to practice every night, and I did. It was that simple. Somehow, it worked. I won. When they called my name, I was stunned. I couldn't speak, because if I did, I would start bawling. Which I didn't understand. How could I be crying about something good? So I stood there in an awkward gray suit my mother had forced me to wear because she thought it looked "classy" and had my picture taken for the paper with this contorted look on my face—half hidden by glasses.

Mr. Serwacki, my sixth-grade teacher, hung a sign on our classroom door: HOME OF THE CITYWIDE SPEECH CHAMPION. I was embarrassed. I knew it was too much. Things were shifting. I was no longer one of the Cindys.

At the gifted program I attended, I overheard a girl who had been in the speech-contest with me say, "She only won because her mother's on the school committee." All my hard work reduced to one sentence. And maybe that *was* the only reason I won. I'll never know.

I've often joked—and there is always some truth to jokes—that I peaked in sixth grade. And sometimes I believe it. I don't know that I've been as successful since. Something changed after that year. Who *was* that person who had the audacity to assume she should be president? Where did that confidence come from? And that self-discipline? Who *was* that person who was able to say I want this and then make it happen?

Was it the glasses?

Or was it me?

Marissa Walsh

Man in the Mirror

As class president, my job at the sixth-grade "graduation" was to welcome the parents. Even though I had won the speech contest, I fumbled my words. My self-confidence, pierced by that girl, had started to deflate. I redeemed myself slightly by starring in a skit called *16 Minutes: Barbara Walnut*. But even though I had my own skit, I desperately wanted to be part of the cool number: the choreographed dance to Michael Jackson's "Thriller," complete with fog machine. I wanted to be wearing parachute pants, not my speech-contest suit. But every GWG knows that glasses and fog don't mix.

The Sergio Valente Pair

1984 ~ 1986

Anastasia Krupnik was ten. She had . . . glasses with large owl-eyed rims, which she had chosen herself at the optician's.

—*Anastasia Krupnik,* LOIS LOWRY

The Purchase

I obviously could not start junior high wearing the glasses I had worn since the third grade. Especially now that I was a full-time girl with glasses. I was starting at a new school with new kids; it seemed important to make a good first impression. Another trip to Mr. Specs with my mother was in order.

This time I headed straight to the adult section and chose a trendy "designer" pair by Sergio Valente. (It was the eighties.) They felt more adult, more sophisticated—more junior high. In fact they were reminiscent of the glasses Dustin Hoffman wore in *Tootsie* when he transformed himself from Michael Dorsey into Dorothy Michaels. Wearing them, I also looked like I was in drag. They clashed with my braces, my long straight homemade-ribbon-barretted hair, my corduroy skirts, my knee socks. My preppy schoolgirl garb hadn't caught up to my glasses.

I'm sure my mother probably encouraged me to try on other pairs. But when a GWG makes up her mind about something, it is virtually impossible to sway her. I had decided this was the right pair for me. I may not have had a wrist full of Swatches or a Benetton rugby like many of my classmates (I had the uncool and more affordable Coca-Cola version instead), but I insisted on my designer Sergio Valente glasses.

These frames were clear plastic with a subtle purple tint. They were not for children. And, though seemingly impossible, they were even bigger than my first pair. In fact, my face was barely visible. The nifty swirly silver decorative earpieces would have been right at home on Sophia Loren. Instead of approaching the ear from the top, they came from below. Hard to explain. Sort of like junior high.

The most exciting thing about them, however, was the case they came in. It was made out of denim, or "dunga-ree," as my mother called it, with the Sergio Valente logo on it. It almost made up for not having an actual pair of Sergio Valente jeans.

Black Eye

As a full-time GWG, I acquired a full-time bully. She and I had been friends since the summer before first grade, and it was she who introduced me to *The Official Preppy Handbook* and Hello Kitty, for which I am forever grateful. We didn't go to the same school until fourth grade, when she switched from Catholic to public, and then we were in the same class. The summer before, I tutored her in math, because they were behind us at her old school and I wanted her to be caught up. I didn't know why she was switching schools, but I assumed it was because her parents were getting a divorce. She was the first kid I knew whom this had happened to, but I had overheard a lot of yelling and screaming when I was at her house, so I wasn't surprised.

Things changed when she got to my school. I already had my school friends, and she was always getting in trouble. We grew apart. But in seventh grade, at our new school, she went on the attack. There, we were all starting with a blank slate. People didn't know me—or her—yet. And while my former classmates hadn't seen me as a GWG, I was afraid my new classmates wouldn't be able to see past it. Every day, at lunch, in homeroom, in the few classes we had together, my bully would make fun of me.

I told my parents. They told me what every parent in the history of parenting has said to a child at one time or another: (1) Feel sorry for her. (2) She's obviously jealous of you. (3) Put yourself in her shoes. (4) Ignore her. (5) She *wants* you to respond. They said all the things that parents say but that don't really help when you're twelve.

Eventually, I challenged her to a fight. This is how things were done in junior high. It took place in my side yard. My brother broke it up before she was able to remove my glasses. Without them, I was Piggy—a goner. But she probably hadn't read *Lord of the Flies*.

I'll See You in My Dreams

I started wearing my Sergios to bed. I hated those first few minutes of fumbling blindness when I woke up in the morning or during the night. I would pretend that I had simply fallen asleep while reading rather than admit I was sleeping with them on. On his way to bed my father would try to pry them gently from my face.

Things I Wasn't Supposed to See

1. In my old neighborhood, a kid went up the hill and came back down with a ten-speed bike. Didn't say anything. Found out later it had been stolen.

2. Santa Claus present: a bike hidden in my grandparents' cellar. It was covered with a blanket.

3. *Are You There God? It's Me, Margaret.* Read it in third grade. Too young.

4. *You Can't Do That on Television* at my grandparents' house. (My parents refused to get cable, my mother didn't like the green slime.)

5. Episode of *Wonder Woman* where an evil scientist sucked the brains out of the tops of people's heads with a machine. With the babysitter. Couldn't sleep.

6. *Taps* at my parents' friends' house. I felt sick afterward.

7. *Redbook* magazine, until I asked my grandmother

in front of everyone if she had gone through menopause yet. Then the magazines went up on top of the refrigerator, out of reach.

8. A girl selling drugs to another girl, in junior high.

Bright Eyes

I met Katie on the French class field trip to Quebec in seventh grade. I didn't take French, but my mother asked if I could go anyway, and I did.

I've always been confused and intrigued by how friendship works. It seemed easier in elementary school, or maybe it just didn't matter as much then. But in junior high it felt like I had lost the instruction manual. I got Super Honor Roll, but I couldn't figure this thing out. I found an old copy of *How to Win Friends and Influence People* at my grandparents' house, but it seemed too contrived. Either people liked you or they didn't. You couldn't force it.

But with Katie it was easy. I could talk to her. The timing was right—we were both in need of a best friend—and we had a lot in common. We both had two younger siblings, went to the same church, and were Girl Scouts. She was loud and funny and a bit crude, the kind of girl who would do or say anything. And she saw past my knee-socked exterior.

She had one of those comfortable family rooms, with deep leather couches that took up three of the walls and, most important, cable! I did not have cable. I did not have MTV. But Katie did, and we watched Dweezil Zappa and drank orange soda and ate peanut M&M's and rented *The Breakfast Club* and *The Sure Thing*. I was there all the time. Her parents didn't seem to mind.

She introduced me to taking the bus to the mall on Saturdays and to those little stores that were cropping up (or maybe they were always there) that catered to teenage girls. She introduced me to celebrity crushes ("I heart Corey Hart!" "I heart Emilio Estevez!"), *Seventeen* magazine, passing notes in the hall, and the book *Me Me Me Me Me* by M. E. Kerr, which made me feel rebellious and cool, like her. She was what Anne of Green Gables would have described as a kindred spirit. I had finally found one. I thought maybe it was what having a sister felt like. It helped, of course, that we both wore glasses.

Through the Looking Glass

The summer between seventh and eighth grades I attended a musical-theater workshop. I was one of the youngest kids, but I was the tallest girl, so I was cast in our musical production of *Alice in Wonderland* to play Alice when she was big. The shortest girl was cast as small (normal) Alice. We looked absolutely nothing alike. She had short blond hair. I had long brown hair. I wore glasses. She did not. So when Alice grew, she developed a vision problem. The directors, a husband and wife team (aren't they always?), asked if I'd be willing to play the part without my glasses. People who don't wear glasses don't get that they are necessary. That we literally *cannot see* without them.

I said no.

When it was time for me to switch with Small Alice, genie-type music would play, and I would swish into the curtain and she would swish out. We would not be replacing *Cats* anytime soon.

There was a cute high school boy in the workshop. He may have been the only boy; he's the only one I remember, anyway. We had a scene where we had to dance together. I had never danced with a boy before. It made me blush, and after the show one of my relatives asked if he was my boyfriend.

I still don't know if I was cast as Alice because I was good or simply because I was the tallest girl. I abandoned acting shortly thereafter.

For Your Eyes Only

At the beginning of eighth grade, a boy noticed me, even with my glasses. Maybe even because of them. But I had been blind to what was really going on. Or maybe I hadn't let myself see.

Wendy passed me a note during English. The note read "Do you like Kevin?" and even though—believe me—I did, I wrote back no, that Kevin and I were friends from way back when he was on my brother's baseball team. It was true. I was there when he hit his first home run. The only reason I said this was because I knew Wendy's best friend, Laureen, liked him too.

I winced a bit when I saw Kevin and Laureen slow dancing to "Purple Rain" at the next dance, but I knew I had made my bed. I lay in it. A lot.

Rose hadn't gone through the kind of John Hughes metamorphosis where she shed her glasses, got a good haircut, and the football captain fell in love with her at the prom.

—*In Her Shoes,* JENNIFER WEINER

The Invisible Pair

1986 ~ 1990

The Purchase

Contact lenses, like most things in eighth grade, came about in part because Katie wanted a pair. "Should I get blue contacts???!" she asked me in a note. I was happy with just regular.

At the end of seventh grade I got my braces off. In January of eighth grade I got my ears pierced by my grandmother's hairdresser, Michael. And in March I got contacts.

I was shy, at least with people I didn't know, and with authority figures especially, but somehow I squeaked out to the eye doctor that I was interested in contacts.

He turned on me. "Why do you want contacts?" he barked. "You don't think boys will like you with glasses? Is that all you care about? How you look?" Well, it wasn't *all* I cared about. But yes, I did care. I wanted boys to like me. I was thirteen. But he made me feel ashamed. I told my mother.

My mother is not one of those pushy, aggressive moms. But you'd better not make her children feel bad. Especially if you're a doctor. She had words with him, and that was the last he saw of us.

To be fair, there *was* a practical reason for contacts (the one my nonfrivolous parents had used to make their decision): sports. I played softball, basketball, and three seasons of soccer; my fears of getting hit in the face were justified. My brother Steven played baseball, basketball, and soccer. He had tried the Kareem Abdul-Jabbar sports goggles for a while, but can you imagine anything worse for a thirteen-year-old girl? I really didn't need anyone to start calling me Kareem. Or Abdul. Or Jabbar.

Steven and I were in this together. Since we were the only people in the family who needed to go to an eye doctor, and the decline in our eyesight had begun at the same time, our eye care was linked. If he got contacts, I got contacts.

Mom called our trusted, competent, and bespectacled pediatrician for a referral. He sent us to his own eye doctor, in Boston, who didn't have any problem with kids our age getting contacts.

We sat at a table in his office while his assistant taught us how to insert and remove and—most important—clean the contact lenses. Steven was done in five minutes and ready to leave, while I was still trying to get my finger close enough to my eye to put the contact in. I didn't want to pop my eyeball out or do other irreparable damage. You'd think Steven, who had been the victim of an eye injury in elementary school that required him to wear an eye patch for a few weeks, would have been more concerned.

Were we *supposed* to be putting our fingers in our eyes? Was the eyeball *meant* to be touched? Did my eyes really *want* little pieces of plastic on top of them?

In my case the answer was a resounding no.

My new glasses may have been invisible, but I could still feel them—I knew they were there.

Contacts Accoutrements

1. Saline solution
2. Case
3. Enzyme tablets
4. Little cups for the enzyme treatment
5. Eye drops
6. Short fingernails
7. Two paper cups filled with water if you stay over somewhere unprepared

Glasses Accoutrements

1. Nose

You'll Put Your Eye Out

At home by myself, I couldn't get the contacts in, and I certainly couldn't get them out (much harder!). I was too lazy to clean them, and I had an uncanny ability to lose them down the sink drain and on the floor. "Don't walk in here!" I would cry frantically as I searched the blue bathroom tiles. As if that weren't bad enough, either I rubbed too hard when I was cleaning them or I would snag one on the edge of my fingernail and tear it.

At school, everyone knew about my new contacts. "It's going to be so weird seeing Marissa without glasses," one of the boys told Katie. The daughter of our former principal told me the rules for putting on eye makeup with contacts. Ms. Hegan, my algebra teacher and fellow contact-lens wearer, empathized with my adjustment process and let me go to the girls' bathroom during class so I could try to fix my misbehaving contact with saline solution. She didn't bother giving me a hall pass—she knew I wouldn't fool around. I was self-conscious about it, though; I didn't want people to think I was using my sore eyes as a way to get attention, or to get out of class.

Before contacts, I never went into the bathroom at school, not even if I was having my period. Things happened in there you didn't want to know about. That day, I walked in and ran into a girl I knew but was not friends with. She was crying and seemed to be having trouble breathing. I went out into the hallway and flagged down our gym teacher, Ms. Foster, who happened to be walking by. She came in and immediately got the girl to start taking deep breaths into someone's brown paper lunch bag. I left, shaken up. What had happened to make the girl so upset? I never found out. In fact, I never spoke to her again. This was a side of junior high I had never seen before.

My torn contacts hurt, but at least I could remove them.

Sight Gag

Because of all the trouble I was having, the eye doctor asked me to return to the office for a second instructional session. I needed extra help. I had failed at contact lenses. It was the second thing (baseball was the first) that my brother was actually better at than I. What was happening?

I was lucky. My parents were patient and, for some reason, kept replacing my lost and torn contacts. Why didn't I just throw in the towel? I should have given up right then and there and claimed my fate. I was a Girl with Glasses. But I was too young to know better. It felt like the glasses were in the way.

Most Blind

The week before the eighth-grade dance we voted for "superlatives": Most Popular, Prettiest, Most Likely to Succeed. Eighth-grade graduation seemed too early to be able to make these judgments about our peers. I mean, we were thirteen. I already had my suspicions about who might win Most Wanted someday, but I wasn't really sure how to measure success.

Even though we had superlatives, we did not have a prom. What we had was strictly referred to as a dance, and it was held in the gym we shared with the elementary school next door. My mother refused to let me wear a prom-style dress, even though some of the girls were wearing Gunne Sax and had dates and had rented limos and were eating at Tai Hong beforehand. My "date" was Katie, and my "chauffeur" was my father. My dress was a two-piece white-and-blue-striped summer outfit that my mother loved and felt was "appropriate." I hated it. It seemed plain and babyish and too casual, especially among the spaghetti straps and taffeta.

But the real fashion emergency involved my hair. In some misguided attempt to create curls, I had braided my hair a few days earlier and left the braids in until just an hour before I was scheduled to leave. I had never left braids in for that long. When I undid the braids, my hair was standing up straight frizzy, Bride of Frankenstein style. I couldn't be seen in public.

My parents stifled their laughter (tragedy was often met with laughter in my house) and sprang into action. My mother told me to wet and comb my hair. My father called Katie and told her we were running late. Somehow the two of them got me into the car, and then Katie got me out of the car and into the dance.

I didn't slow-dance with a boy—none of my close friends did. We fast-danced with each other, declared that we were going to "fight for our right to party," hand-gestured to Prince's "I Will Die 4 U," and thought we were missing out during the interminable "Stairway to Heaven" closer. When the superlative winners list was posted on the wall, I didn't run over to see if I was on it. I remained calm and disinterested. I remember someone telling me, and then wanting to go and confirm it for myself. If it hadn't been crowded, I would have read the list over and over

Marissa Walsh

again and tried to commit it to memory for further analysis later. But there were too many people pressing forward, and I didn't want to call any more attention to myself. I hated my dress, my hair was a mess, and I was Class Brain.

Secretly I was glad. I was the smartest and I wanted to be recognized for that. But the other part of me, the girl who had almost stayed home because of her hair, the girl who had switched to contacts, the girl who should have been at the dance with Kevin, would have preferred something—anything—else. Best At Soccer or Most Resembles Molly Ringwald or Most Likely to Succeed. I mean, isn't it safe to assume that the Class Brain *is* the most likely to succeed? But that title was given to someone with the shoo-in-for-Class-Brain last name Smart.

If Katie had been given a superlative, it would have been Funniest or Most Outrageous or Most Likely To Be on *Saturday Night Live*. I would have killed for any of those. My glasses may now have been out of sight, but it didn't matter—I was still Class Brain. I was still the girl with glasses.

The Better to See You with, My Dear

That summer, I was hired as a "page" at the Lynn Public Library in downtown Lynn. As an official contact-lens wearer, I was lucky to get the job. Not every librarian is a GWG, but in a 2004 survey of three thousand eyeglass wearers and nonwearers conducted by Essilor International, 74 percent chose "librarian" as a profession associated with wearing eyeglasses—more than any other profession.

Being a page entailed reshelving books, alphabetizing and shifting shelves, and retrieving books from the closed stacks. Before Google, there was me.

I don't remember expressing any interest in getting the job, but I was switching from public to private school that September, so I needed to make money. Plus, my parents probably wanted to get me out of the house. But, like most GWGs, I loved being around books all day.

Don't It Make My Brown Eyes Blue

Ashley was not her real name. Her real first name was Jennifer, but on the first day of freshman orientation at my private school, she refused to answer to it. We were out on the field, waiting to engage in some sort of trust-building we're-all-going-to-be-friends orientation exercise while they called the roll. "Jennifer?" No one answered. "Jennifer?" We all looked around. *Bueller?* I wanted to raise my hand, just to end the tension. Which one of us was Jennifer?

Finally, Jennifer spoke up. She was a slight girl with a rather large head. In a high-pitched British accent that sounded fake, she said, "It's Ashley, actually. My name is Ashley." Everyone looked at each other. Was she kidding? Sadly, she was not. It had only been a few hours, but we could all breathe a sigh of relief that at least there would be someone lower down on the ninth-grade totem pole than us.

I wish Ashley/Jennifer had figured out that it's okay to have secrets. Wearing contact lenses, for example. It is something about you that nobody needs to know. You can decide whom and when and if to tell. You can control this information. Unlike almost everything else in high school.

The View

The only GWGs at my high school were on the faculty. (It took me until senior year, unfortunately, to fully embrace the fact that they were the people I had the most in common with.) I never wore my glasses to school. Ever. I spent my entire high school career as a girl without glasses.

I had chosen the school, in part, because I was drawn in by the catalog and its black-and-white photos of intelligent-looking students. During my school tour, I fell in love with the school building, an old mansion made of stone with white columns, and the grounds—there was a pond, and acres of green fields and trees. We were in horse country, far from Lynn's urban landscape. It seemed like the kind of place a GWG would go.

I was wrong.

And I didn't know anything about private school. I

didn't know that most of the kids would be coming from other private schools and would already know each other. I didn't know anybody. I didn't know there were private schools that weren't high schools. I didn't know what L.L.Bean or Manchester G&T was. I had bought new school clothes that would have been cool at the public high school—Esprit, The Limited—but at this school they were completely wrong.

The school was far enough away that you had to drive to get there. A lot of the kids drove themselves.

There were a few other kids from Lynn, and none of us drove yet or had a car, so our parents formed a carpool. Our carpool was actually too big for one car, but we were from Lynn, so we were inclusive and all squeezed in and sat on laps. The Lynn carpool was responsible for most of the school's diversity quota: one Latino, one Jamaican American, one African American, one hockey player, two urban middle class. They should have paid to get us there.

When it was my father's turn, he insisted on driving his gigantic brown boat of a car with heat that barely worked and only AM radio. As a teenage girl with glasses hiding behind contacts I was embarrassed, but he felt it was important for the rich kids to see that the world was made up of all kinds of cars. Cars, he said, were for getting from point A to point B.

I had thought starting high school as a non-glasses-wearing girl would feel liberating; I had thought I would fit in and appear to be just like everybody else. But with my father's car and my clothes and my address and my carpool, that was impossible. Maybe Class Brain hadn't been so bad after all.

Ways of Seeing

My first non-Alice dance with a boy was to Madonna's "Crazy For You." It was with this hockey player who had gone to my school but left in tenth grade, and it was at a dance at Katie's school. Katie had told him to ask me to dance, and he had. "Eye to eye we need no words at all." But during the dance I kept saying that I felt like an idiot, which I did, because Katie had had to ask him, but he thought I was saying I felt like an idiot for dancing with him. At the time, I couldn't see it—or myself—from his perspective.

Boy Watching

PETER #1:

Peter #1 drove me up the causeway to what he affectionately referred to as "the Front." The Front was the entrance to the parking lot at the beach where I would be working as a "laborer" the summer after tenth grade. Since it was my first day of work, I was sitting in the cab of the pickup truck. I didn't realize then that I would be spending the rest of the summer corralled in the back, trying to perch nonchalantly on the edge while images of my brain—splattered all over the ground—ran through it. My job consisted of taking the parking lot money, picking up trash on the beach, and "maintaining" the two public bathrooms.

I still worked a few shifts at the library, but this was better money. And it was at the beach. I was attempting to put my girl-with-glasses days behind me.

Peter #1 was the boss. He decided your fate for the day: Would I be stuck cleaning the bathrooms, or would I be at the Front, collecting money and sunbathing? The already-tan college girls would flirt with him to get the parking lot spots. They would wear bikini tops under their job-issued T-shirts and take the shirts off at precisely the right moment. This was before skin cancer. I didn't own a bikini, so I often found myself cleaning the bathrooms, which I actually didn't mind because when I was finished I could just read.

I was queasy about emptying the sanitary-napkin bin, though—why is it that everyone at the beach seems to have their period?—so Peter #1 did it for me. I'd often find myself riding alone with him, and he would drive slowly through the parking lot while checking out the scenery. "Hey, baby," he would say out the window, and I would wonder what these "babies" thought about me, sitting there with him. And sometimes he would ask me what I thought about them.

HENRY: Henry was a supervisor. And Katie's science teacher. She would come visit me at work so she could see him. But I got to call him by his first name. He was also a body-builder and wore gray sweatpants to work every single day, even when it was ninety-eight degrees. There was much speculation as to why.

PETER #2: Peter #2 was in charge of the parking lot. He sat on the other side of me that first day in the truck. I was staring down at my naked white thighs. They looked fat to me, the way most thighs do when they are smashed against a vinyl seat in the middle of summer, and this concerned me, because I already had a crush on Peter #2. I was the new girl, trying to get names straight and they were teasing me. "Hi, I'm Peter," Peter #2 said when he got in. Peter #1 looked at him. "No, I'm Peter." I looked to one and then the other, confused. I wasn't good at this. "What's your real name?" I finally asked Peter #2, and then when it really was Peter, I felt like an idiot.

Peter #2 was smart and sensitive : every GWG's dream. He had short blond hair and round silver eyeglasses and always wore black Converse high-tops with his black concert T-shirts and cut-off Dickies. He was a college student in D.C. and was into bands I had never heard of. He actually used to request me at the Front a lot, which I of course assumed meant he liked me, but it was really because I was smart and he knew I didn't steal money. I would take those opportunities to talk to him about the things we had in common: a penchant for wearing black, mostly, and the fact that he had gone to my brother's high school. We would discuss movies and music, too, but mainly we gossiped about the people we worked with. Sometimes we would eat lunch together—he always ate peanut butter and jelly—and I would tell him about the books I was reading. He gave me a Dead Milkmen hat once, and he tried to get me into an eighteen-plus show at a club in Boston. On his last day of work he kissed me good-bye on the cheek, and I walked to my mother's car clutching my face like Marcia Brady did when Davy Jones kissed hers. But I knew he got giddy around one of the college girls who left to go back to school early. She was preppy, bouncy, and blond, and when I put two and two together I thought, *Not you, too, Peter. Not you.*

HARRY: When Peter #2 heard that Harry would be joining us that summer, he resurrected a saying of Harry's that had been passed down from one generation of beach workers to the next: "A beached jellyfish is a dead jellyfish." Harry played hockey.

DICK: Dick writhed around behind his sunglasses, his head covered in a white sailor hat, as he described how he was eating a girl out (his words) until he was interrupted by the arrival of her parents. We were supposed to be picking up trash in the parking lot, but he and the cool kids were leaning against the wall, waiting until Peter #1 and the truck appeared to actually do any work. I was pretending to read, but I was actually listening very intently. Dick

Marissa Walsh

was still in high school too, but, because chicks dug him (his words), he was the self-proclaimed leader of our little group. We worked when he worked; we stopped when he stopped. Peter #1 had hit on his sister the previous summer, and Dick was still pissed off about it. One day he found a roach in the parking lot, and he and his entourage smoked it during lunch. Of course, there was too little left for any of them to have gotten high, but he acted all stoned anyway when he got back. He was addicted to Advil—claimed he liked the taste—and was always trying to start something with one of the lifeguards. The thing about Dick was that he was a small guy, short and skinny, and I could have taken him. But he was also funny, and I laughed at his jokes in spite of myself. When I worked the Front with him, he would take money from cars, not give them a receipt, and pocket the cash. I would shake my head at him, and next thing he'd be sticking cash in my shorts pockets. In front of everyone he would ask what I was reading, and I knew he was making fun of me. But at the end of the summer he showed up with *A Farewell to Arms* in his back pocket, and I was strangely attracted to the asshole.

MIKE: Mike was the other quiet one. We spent many silent hours together. He did love those Red Sox, though, and knew all this useless baseball trivia which he would discuss with Peter #2, who also loved the Sox even though he was punk rock. Mike was also very funny and would make pointed subversive comments under his breath that usually only I would hear. One day we were working together, not talking, at the bathhouse. He was sitting on the railing of the fence outside, and I could see up the leg of his shorts. He was wearing briefs.

TOM: "Honey, I need the mop!" Tom the Satanist screamed from the doorway of the women's side of the halfway house, an aptly named restroom halfway between the beginning of the beach—marked by the Tides Restaurant, with its take-out window contributing to the thousands of salt, pepper, and ketchup packets littering the ground—and the bathhouse, another aptly named building, as the boys often had to do a check of the men's showers. "Thanks, baby," he said as I handed it to him. I swooned. No one had ever called me baby before. We'd be riding in the truck, whenever we were lucky enough to get seats up front, and that James Taylor song would come on, the one about Carolina, and Tom would turn it up, sigh, and say, "This is Jessica's favorite song. She's from North Carolina." And I would nod and make a mental note to hate that song from then on. They had just graduated from Phillips Andover together, which meant that they had had sex, because it was a boarding school and everyone in boarding school had had sex. He was heading to NYU in the fall to study film.

Peter #2 loved him too. I had loved Peter #2 first, in the way you love a particularly young, good-looking teacher. But Tom was a peer; he inspired different feelings. Peter #2 used to fawn over Tom and go on to me about how smart he was. "I've never been able to talk to an eighteen-year-old about Heidegger or the Clash before," he would say. I wouldn't say anything.

Tom had been a late addition to our work crew. His charisma rivaled Dick's, and they hated each other immediately. We misfits made him our leader. He would make fun of Dick, sometimes right to his face, but in a subtle way that Dick didn't pick up on. I guess the Satanism came out after a few weeks. It was Tom's secret weapon, the thing that really turned the tide his way. Even the college girls were giggling about it. Tom would find dead fish on the beach and enlist Harry to spread the word and insinuate that he may have been behind it. I don't know if he did it only to get Dick's attention, but it worked. Dick was hooked. Tom had him eating out of the palm of his hand. He brought in *The Satanic Bible* to show Dick, and I was afraid to look at it, but Dick brought it home and read the whole thing.

I don't know if Tom was really a Satanist—I don't think he was, I think he just wanted to fuck with Dick. One time

Harry, Mike, Tom, and I drove to his house for lunch, and I thought, *What if they overpower me and perform some satanic ritual?* But they didn't.

CHARLIE: . . . Always sunburned.

Blindsided

The day we found out about Mr. Keating, Guy wasn't in Algebra 2/Trig. He had ditched, and I had a vision of him driving to Mr. Keating's house. And I wished he had thought to ask me to go with him. There had been an all-school meeting, and what was said—drugs, problem, resigned, help—was foggy, and so much was left unsaid, and we all had questions, but we had to go to classes. I was a senior, and Mr. Keating was the senior-class advisor. Mrs. L, the kind school counselor, was on hand if anyone needed to talk, and it was generally understood that if people needed space they could have it. Which is why Guy wasn't in algebra.

Somehow I made it through the day by not talking about it at all. I just ignored the whole thing. I thought it was weird that I wasn't upset, but things had been different with Mr. Keating, and this actually explained a lot.

Before school started, the senior class went to the woods in Maine for a week of trust-building exercises, camping out, forced bonding, and leadership skill–building through ropes-courses. It was fun for other people. To me it was one of the worst things about private school. (Each year had its own version.) There's a picture of me from the trip sitting on a dock with a terrible look on my face, as if I smelled something bad.

The week has certain traditions, one of which is that one of the nights is spent camping on an island, to which you are required to row. Here I caught a few breaks:

1. I wasn't in the group that got stranded on the island.

2. Because the other group got stranded, my group didn't even have to go to the island; we got to camp out on the beach instead.

3. My best friend, Tricia, was in my group.

4. Mr. Keating was our chaperone.

I assumed at least this part would be good—Mr. Keating was fun and in a band (they used to play our dances) and had brought his guitar on the trip. Plus, he didn't put up with the cliquey crap. I was happily looking forward to a kooky Beatles sing-along around the campfire. But Mr. Keating wasn't really around. He kept disappearing, and when he finally showed up, he made what felt like a half-hearted attempt at playing a few songs and singing before calling it a night. He said he was going to sleep right on the beach next to the campfire under the stars and urged us to do the same. Tricia and I were hot and claustrophobic in our tent, so we took Mr. Keating's advice and put our sleeping bags on the beach next to his. We woke up the next morning wet and covered in bug bites. He was gone.

Looking back on it, there were plenty of signs. He'd been our assistant softball coach the previous spring, but his attendance at practice had been erratic. He stopped traveling with the team to away games and made lame excuses why. He showed up wearing sunglasses to a game in Boston and said that he had just been to the eye doctor. But hadn't he also been wearing sunglasses at a basketball game that winter—inside?

He had been my ninth-grade English teacher and the only teacher that year who had really seen me. When he became my class's advisor, he invited the entire class over to his house for a cookout. I had never been to a teacher's house before. We knew his wife and baby. He had boundless energy, and he ran the Social Committee and organized raucous events like Halloween and a casino night and something called the Magical Mystery Tour that was an overnight happening I didn't go on. But I went to the other events, because the fact that he was in charge made them cooler and more inclusive. The Social Committee was a band of followers, including me. It was a motley group of groupless people, and he was our Pied Piper. He used to let me hang out in his office, in a stuffed green chair, even when he wasn't there. Being in with him sometimes made it okay that for a while I wasn't in with anyone else.

The day we found out, my father picked me up from carpool. The minute I closed the door behind me, I burst into tears.

I never saw Mr. Keating again.

Now You See It, Now You Don't

One night I was following a friend to a party but when we got there we decided we didn't really want to go in so we got back in our respective cars and she pulled up to turn around and I blindly followed her but it was dark and I heard a sound as I was backing up. A cat? It hadn't been visible. Had I hit it? I got out of the car to check, but I couldn't see anything.

The Spare Pair

1988~1990

ZACH: *"You're not wearing your glasses."*

LANE: *"That's right."*

ZACH: *"But you're blind without your glasses."*

LANE: *"The wonder of contacts."*

ZACH: *"Contacts?"*

LANE: *"Contacts."*

ZACH: *"Why?"*

—*Gilmore Girls*

The Purchase

I may have become a girl without glasses, but I still wore them at night after removing my contacts. The Sergios had run their course, however; I think one earpiece was hanging on by a Band-Aid. I needed a less embarrassing backup pair. Especially since I was now a licensed driver. My parents agreed.

I had outgrown Mr. Specs, so we tried Banville Optical in Salem, the next city over. They had a new, slightly larger selection. But how do you shop for glasses you never expect to wear in public? They need to be acceptable enough, just in case there is ever a contact-lens emergency and you are forced to wear them. But you don't want them to be too good, because then you will feel guilty for not wearing them more often—or at all. I picked a pair of round tortoise-shell wire-rimmed glasses which today could be described with two words: Harry Potter. They were the complete opposite of the Sergios. And my brother Steven chose the same pair. We went to different schools, so there was never the chance we would be seen together. And he never wore his anyway.

During my last semester of high school, Steven and I both caught chicken pox at the same time from our younger brother, Joseph. We had teased him while he scratched, and just when we thought we were in the clear, we got what we deserved. We took over the living room in our bathrobes and glasses and watched movies; Steve on one couch, me on the other. We moaned and groaned and passed the calamine lotion back and forth, grateful for our spare pairs, and each other.

Open Your Eyes

I still have a note I wrote to Katie in junior high. "For Katie's Eyes ONLY!!!" is written on the top, but instead of the word *eyes*, I drew a pair of eyes, with glasses. I never gave it to her.

One afternoon during the summer between tenth and eleventh grades, I called her when I got home from work, per usual, and her little sister answered. When I asked for Katie, her sister said, "Just a minute," and then, without covering the phone, asked, "Where should I tell her you are?" When she got back on the phone and said, "Katie's not home," I hung up. She sounded confused. So was I.

Katie called me the next day during dinner and said she wanted to talk about it. I told her I was eating but would call her later. I never did. As is often the case in these situations, I was as mad at myself as I was at her. Why had I been so stupid? Why hadn't I been able to see?

She went to a big, normal high school and had a large group of friends, most of whom lived nearby. I went to a tiny, abnormal high school and had a few friends, all of whom lived far away. She had understandably gotten tired of playing cruise director and including me in her social life. I needed her more than she needed me.

By not calling back and accepting her explanation, I suppose I cut off my own nose to spite my face. (Luckily I was wearing contacts.) Maybe we could have worked things out. But to be honest, we had been growing apart. She was the funny one, the loud one, the one in the spotlight. I'd always been the sidekick—Marcie to her Peppermint Patty. But that wasn't really who I was anymore. I didn't want to be the second choice. The spare.

Eyewitness

My new boss at the beach had a mustache and wore a park ranger's uniform. It was my third summer, the one before college, and Peter #2 and I were the only two left. I was wearing my glasses to work—I didn't care—and one day I had this conversation:

New Boss: "Look at those fags. How disgusting."

Me: "Uh, just because there happen to be two men together doesn't mean that they're gay—"

New Boss: "Oh, yeah? So, which way do you swing?"

Me: "Excuse me?"

New Boss: "Are you gay? Is that why you love them so much?"

Peter said New Boss probably thought we were both gay because we wore glasses. "He's intimidated by us," he said, "because we wear glasses and are smarter than he is."

I wanted to believe him.

But when I told Peter I was afraid my eyesight would continue to get worse until I was eventually blind, he told me a story about frogs and lily pads to illustrate it would never happen, that it didn't make any sense. Or make me feel better.

Sight for Sore Eyes

Some GWGs (Hillary Rodham Clinton, Erica Jong) wear glasses but then switch to contacts. Some GWGs (me) wear contacts but then switch to glasses. And some GWGs (Janet Reno) just wear glasses.

By the end of my senior year of high school I didn't care anymore. I had gotten into college early-decision. I had become close with many of my teachers. I was happy with the schoolwork I was doing. I had survived high school. I wore—gasp!—glasses to my last final exam. One of my teachers noticed and said, "Are those real? They make you look smart." He favored bow ties.

I wore them off and on that summer, then officially switched back to glasses during my first semester of college. I wish I could say it represented a triumphant return to my GWG roots. Over the summer it had. It had been about a new confidence, a renewed sense of identity. But that first semester, at my GWG college, it was partly about laziness. I had worn my contacts at first, but once classes started, I quickly became one of those jeans-sweatshirt-Birkenstocks-glasses-ponytail-only-break-the-contacts-out-for-parties-where-boys-might-be-present girls. It became too much work to clean them and put them in and take them out.

And it was about other things too. My roommate wore glasses, but she barely spoke to me and took over our room with her tapestries, allergies, and Joni Mitchell. I had been a big fish in a small, familiar pond the year before. Now I was in a bigger, foreign pond, and I wasn't just small; I had forgotten how to swim.

It was obviously time for a new prescription.

DARIA: *"Do you think contacts reveal the you-ness inside?"*

JANE: *"I don't know. Who's Eunice and why doesn't she get her own body?"*

—*Daria*

The Sparer Pair

1991

The (Un-)Purchase

Second semester of my first year of college, the plastic "tortoise shell" on The Spare Pair cracked and began to come off. Could things get any worse? But they weren't broken. And I could see that underneath the fake tortoise was plain silver wire. I removed all the plastic and had "new" silver frames! A silver lining, literally, had been revealed.

During spring break, I visited Katie at NYU. She had written me or I had written her. Her name was Kate now. We drank Rolling Rock beer, ate Dum Dum lollipops, went to the St. Patrick's Day parade, stood in line for *Saturday Night Live* tickets, and saw a midnight showing of *Taxi Driver* at the Angelika with her film-school boyfriend. It wasn't the same. But that was okay.

Seeing Stars

GWGs are sensitive and introspective. Sometimes they can feel overwhelmed. I'm sure Velma could have used someone to talk to. She must have had stuff to get off her chest: Scooby and Shaggy's incompetence, the fact that she was the only one of the five who did anything and no one appreciated her, Fred's blind devotion to the Mystery Machine—and Daphne.

I had started having panic attacks that summer. I didn't know what a panic attack was, so I didn't realize that's what was happening. They got worse—debilitating—during my first semester of college. I spent a lot of time at my college's Health Services having various tests done, but they couldn't find anything wrong. It wasn't until second semester that someone finally figured it out.

My first therapist was a kind man, reminiscent of Harriet's bespectacled Dr. Wagner. Just talking to him seemed to do the trick. The attacks went away as suddenly as they had come, and my Dr. Wagner gave a seminar for the doctors at Health Services so they would see the symptoms next time. I wasn't sure whether to feel embarrassed or proud.

Miss Me Blind

My mother started getting headaches before I left for college. She assumed my leaving was the reason. Turned out she needed reading glasses. "I am forty-three now," she kept saying. She refused to get the half glasses, though, so for a while she couldn't see anything when she looked up. Finally, she replaced the top half with glass.

I see much
better now
and my eyes hurt.
                    —from "Contact Lenses," AUDRE LORDE

The
Too Cool for School
Pair

1991-1994

The Purchase

I needed to start over, and I did so with new glasses. I thought, and was told, they were cool. But that's what college is all about. You wear glasses you think are cool. You read Kierkegaard, write bad poetry, hang out at an "underground" coffee shop, wear black bras, drink gin and tonics, dance on the roof and get busted by security, go to candlelight vigils, decide you are a Buddhist, boycott Domino's, fall in love, have your heart broken, have it happen again with the same person, have it happen again with a new person, sleep through class, stay up all night, and call each other by your last names, all while thinking you are cool. Too cool for school.

A college friend of mine actually admitted that she had longed for glasses and had worn fake glasses for a period during high school because she wanted to look smarter. Another friend thought glasses were cool and read in the dark deliberately, desperate to weaken her eyes so she'd need them.

Mine were round and covered nearly my entire face. Like Sally Jesse Raphael's but brown. I bought them the summer after my first year of college. I was working as an intern at the State House in Boston and found a store on Beacon Hill that had a wide, collegiate, Boston selection. I tried on every pair but couldn't decide. I was alone. The salesman was stiff, reserved, and unhelpful.

When I picked them up, I still wasn't sure.

I wasn't sure about returning to school, either. I hadn't wanted to go back. But I didn't have a choice. When I got there sophomore year, wearing the new pair, people complimented me. I told myself things were going to be different. And it worked. They were.

Blind Faith

Sophomore year I made good friends. The kind you can trust to take with you when picking out new frames. Which is essential, because, as every GWG knows, trying on new frames involves removing your glasses. But removing my glasses means I am unable to see. How am I supposed to choose what I need for sight without having any?

When I still had contacts, I would wear them specifically for this task. But these days, the only way I can see how prospective frames look is to put my face as close to the mirror as I can get it. Evaluating frames this way is useless, because being that close to the mirror only allows me to see the frames, not how they actually look on my face. As with one of those optical-illusion posters they sell at the mall, you need to back up and take in the whole view for the hidden picture to come into focus. (Not that I can ever make it out anyway.)

Plus, I inevitably bump my head on the wall mirrors, and there are never enough of the counter mirrors, which can only handle one face at a time. When I was younger I used to bend down to them, which meant that, in addition to not providing a complete picture, they only reflected my face from below. Now I boldly bring the mirror up to my face. It doesn't help, but it makes me feel like I am doing something.

Similarly, the hairdresser always asks me to remove my glasses, then asks me questions I can't possibly answer until I fish my glasses out from under the smock. But by then it is too late. There's nothing to do but hope for the best.

Marissa Walsh

Vision of a Kiss

Most high school and college boys are intimidated by the glasses (and what they represent). They don't really know how to kiss yet themselves, so the glasses present an extra obstacle and source of anxiety. For this reason, the GWG's first kiss sometimes doesn't happen until college. Mine didn't happen until sophomore year. And if the GWG goes to a women's college, chances are it will happen with a woman. This possibility had never occurred to me before, but I was fine with it when it did. GWGs are open-minded.

Lights will be on, glasses will be on, but eyes will be closed. At first. Then the GWG will think—she can never stop thinking—*What happens if I open my eyes?* And she will try, and realize it's okay: You can do it with your eyes open, too. But it's harder to focus, maybe, or it feels wrong, like cheating, to be looking at the other person when the other person doesn't know. Then she will remember that episode of *The Brady Bunch* when Bobby has his first kiss with Millicent (whatever happened to her?) and Mr. Brady said it would be like skyrockets and, sure enough, Bobby sees sky-rockets. You will wonder: *Am I seeing skyrockets? What am I supposed to be seeing? What are skyrockets, anyway? I am seeing nothing; my eyes are closed. Who was Mr. Brady to be giving this advice? I am ridiculous—it was a TV show.* But every time you kiss a new person, you wonder if there are skyrockets, and if there aren't, you think maybe it's something you're doing wrong.

Things That Are Not a Good Idea with Glasses

Roller coasters

Turtlenecks

Masks (ski, Halloween)

Football

Home plate umpire

Rain

Trapeze

Dunking underwater

Snowball fights

Breakdancing

Bette Davis Eyes

At one point I had this thing with someone where mutual attraction had been acknowledged and time was being spent together and flirtatious e-mails were being sent but things just weren't progressing. It was complicated for all sorts of reasons, and I couldn't see a solution, but I decided that if I stopped wearing my glasses, maybe that would make it easier. Maybe if I took away that physical barrier that was within my control, it would make the difference. Maybe it was as simple as this someone never having kissed someone with glasses before, and that was the holdup, and I could do my part to help.

It didn't work.

Staring Contest

A former teacher of mine—a GWG—once told me of her desire, while in college, to throw an entire set of china out her dorm-room window to the pavement below. I looked at her with seventeen-year-old amazement—amazed both that she had had such a desire and that she had admitted to it. Plus, where would she get an entire set of china?

It wasn't until much later, when I myself was in college, that I understood and in fact shared her fantasy. It was the sound I fixated on the most. The crash of delicacy meeting the cold, hard concrete. A soundtrack for nihilism! Oh, the wastefulness! There go the irreplaceable family heirlooms! And I don't give a shit.

The ultimate thrill would have been to do it with our college's china. Elly and I never got that far. We tossed pumpkins from our house's third-floor porch instead. We dropped them and watched with glee as the guts splattered all over the unsuspecting ground. I didn't even think about who would have to clean it up.

I often don't trust myself in department stores. It's only a matter of time, I think, with all that breakable china around, before I start throwing my elbows and knocking vases, decorative plates, and stemware off the shelves, inciting coiffed salesgirls to run after me in a desperate attempt to stop my spree.

It's like being on the roof of a building and getting too close to the edge. First you just peek over, but then you get bolder and see how long you can look before you get vertigo and have to look away. It would be so easy. So easy to just let yourself go. That's why I never go to the edge.

ZACH: *"Why?"*

DAPHNE: *"Velma, do you have a book for every occasion?"*

VELMA: *"Actually, yes."*

—Scooby-Doo and the
Loch Ness Monster

The

Real World Massachusetts

Pair

1994~1996

The Purchase

I was supposed to move to Austin. After graduation. My friend Meliss and me and our stuff in a U-Haul. But Meliss wasn't ready to leave, and my mother was running for state senate and I wanted to be a part of the campaign. Our friends Laura and Britta went to Austin instead. It all worked out.

That September I bought new glasses and my first (and last) adult suit. Light, oval, and silver, the new frames were almost the exact opposite of my college glasses. I guess they were supposed to represent a new beginning. Hard to find at the EyeWorld chain ("the vision professionals") in the North Shore Shopping Center, which, in my *Reality Bites* state, I was forced to patronize for the first (and last) time. I went alone and was obviously in a post-collegiate haze and somehow ended up with pseudo-John Lennon frames. Frames were getting smaller, and oval seemed to be in, but they were the wrong shape for my face, and the silver color didn't suit me. Still, they reflected my situation: a liberal-arts degree, no job, no money, no identity, no idea what to do with my life.

The suit was to wear to an interview in New York. It was from Lord & Taylor and was black. The jacket was big, with shoulder pads, and could be worn either alone or with a blouse underneath. Very *Working Girl*. It wasn't until I was sitting in the chair being interviewed that I crossed my legs and realized the slit in the skirt was still sewn together. I had forgotten to cut it. The thread was visible to both my interviewers. It looked as if I had worn it straight from the store, tags tucked in, and was going to return it as soon as the interview was over. But they either didn't notice, didn't care, or were too kind to draw attention to it. I was surprised that my mother, who was usually on top of these things, hadn't reminded me. I had tried the suit on for her. But she was in the middle of a campaign. And I was not meant to wear suits.

I got the job anyway.

My mother lost the election. Even with my new real-world glasses, I never saw it coming, though almost everyone else had.

Marissa Walsh

See Spot Run

After my mom lost, I applied to be a public school substitute teacher. I wasn't qualified, in the sense that I hadn't taken any education classes and I didn't really like children, but it paid well—fifty bucks a day! And the day was short; it was over at two thirty. GWGs tended to be teachers, librarians, editors, and comedians. I had already worked in a library, I had interviewed for a publishing job and was waiting to hear back, and my parents thought I was a comedian.

Being a sub was my first experience with the world of temporary employment. If they had work, a woman named Pat would call me in the morning, and if I was free (what else did I have to do?), I would say yes. I did not get up and get dressed and sit by the phone, however. I stayed in bed, and if the phone rang my father, the Human Alarm Clock, would answer it and then wake me up. If I wanted to work,

I would get up, go to the phone to receive my assignment, pull on some clothes, and leave. If I didn't want to work, I would wave my father away and roll over. I suppose one way to do it would be to get up early, jog, shower, get dressed, eat breakfast, read the newspaper, and *then* wait for the call. But that just never occurred to me.

Substitute teaching is hard. The people I knew who had done it said it was easy, but they had subbed for high school. In high school you just sit there and read while the kids have a study hall. There is no actual teaching involved. But I was afraid of the older kids. I assumed elementary school would be easier, that the little kids would be cute. Little did I know.

My first job was at my former elementary school, subbing for *my* fifth-grade teacher. Next I had a kindergarten, where the kids sat there like baby birds waiting to be fed, their eyes wide and their mouths open. In a bilingual class I repeated *"Cállate!"* over and over again in my *muy mal* Spanish. Then there was a bad, out-of-control class of all boys. A sub ambush. The principal came and gave them all detention. Finally, after one success in a fourth-grade class, the teacher requested me again the next time she called in sick. (The highest compliment for a sub!) I was happy; her lesson plans were meticulous and easy to follow, and I soon discovered that kids were fine once they got over the novelty of a new person walking in the door. The second time

I showed up, I said, "Good morning, guys!" and they looked up briefly, muttered, "Oh, it's you," and, relieved, went back to what they were doing. I was safe; they knew what to expect with me. We actually got work done.

For some reason the kids couldn't say "Ms.," even though I wrote it on the board. They always called me Mrs., or occasionally Miss, and they would make snowflakes or draw pictures of me, or of the Simpsons, or of themselves, and give them to me at the end of the day, signed, "To Mrs. Walsh." One girl didn't give me a picture but said I looked like Morticia Addams from *The Addams Family*. The principal gave me a pen with the name of the school on it.

The last day of school before Christmas vacation, I subbed for the sixth-grade teacher at the same school as my usual fourth-grade class. I wore my Santa Claus socks and went with the class to sing Christmas carols at a nursing home.

When the fourth-graders spotted me in the hallway at the end of the day, they surrounded and hugged me. I told them that I wouldn't be seeing them again. That I was moving to New York City. "Why would you do that?" one of the girls asked. "What's in New York? We're here." She held on to my leg and wouldn't let go.

Tunnel Vision

I had no job in New York City and no reason to move there, and yet it seemed like time to go. I was getting a little too comfortable in Lynn. Six months after graduation I was still living with my parents, watching reruns of *Beverly Hills, 90210* on Lifetime in the afternoons, and reading all the books I had blown off in college.

It would have been so easy to stay. I didn't *want* to leave. My parents didn't want me to leave. But I knew if I didn't force myself, I never would. It's better to pull the Band-Aid off fast in one motion.

Steven and two of his friends drove me, and one of his friends got all giddy when he saw the skyline: the Empire State Building, the World Trade Center. He was more excited than I was. What had I gotten myself into?

My new roommate wasn't home when I arrived to move in, but the stickers on her door made the fourth-floor

Brooklyn brownstone apartment feel just like college. I may have been entering the real world, but there was a "Don't Fuck With My Vagina" sticker on the entrance.

After the boys had moved me in, I stood at the car's window to say good-bye. They were nervous. They weren't sure about the roommate, the building, the block, Brooklyn. Lynn was a city, but not really. "I don't feel right just leaving you," my brother said. "Are you *sure* you want us to leave you here?" I didn't want them to, but I nodded anyway, and turned away before they could see the tears behind my Real-World-I-Don't-Think-We're-in-Massachusetts-Anymore glasses.

Blind Date

Reality Bites had come out spring semester of my senior year, and I had seen it in town one weekday afternoon by myself when I was probably supposed to be doing something else. I was both terrified and hopeful that my post-graduation life would resemble the film. Oh, for some kooky dancing at the gas-station convenience mart! Drinking games to *Good Times*! A job at the Gap! That cute Winona haircut!

That spring I also met this musician guy at a Liz Phair concert, and he was nice, and I tried to make myself like him so I could get over someone else. We had no chemistry, but I didn't mind. He was in a band. He gave me this really intense bear hug when we parted, even though we had just met. And I soon revealed my "crush" to him, even though my words rang false as soon as they were out of my mouth.

That fall, Musician Guy called me at my parents' and

asked if I had a car I could borrow to help get his band's equipment to a gig. *A gig.* Would this make me a roadie? I said yes. Of course. Musician Guy may have been exploiting my fake crush, but I was bored, and it sounded fun. Who knew? Maybe the band would make it big. And I could say I was with the band. My father told me to watch out for the drugs. But he let me borrow his car.

Meliss had moved to Boston by now—Somerville, to be exact. *Slumerville*, to be more exact. One night Musician Guy and I went to Meliss's to watch *Quadrophenia*, and I drank too much, which I thought would help with Musician Guy—or at least with *Quadrophenia*. I got sick, which never helps with anyone, and poor Meliss held my hair. I wasn't used to drinking with men. But before I got sick, we did have a drunken Store 24 moment: An emaciated man, glasses askew, was lying on the floor. "My Sharona" was not playing.

I would be on the floor soon enough. It was the first time I ever got sick from drinking. Throwing up is a difficult time to be a GWG. You don't really want to be wearing your glasses, but there's just no good place to put them from your vantage point in the bathroom. And you do not want them to fall in. Luckily you are too busy praying for death—and being interrupted by teeth-brushing roommates—to worry about it.

After I moved to New York, Musician Guy sent me a fun

package with the kind of mix tape ("Miss You" by the Stones; "I've Got You Under My Skin" by Frank Sinatra) you dream of getting from someone you like. I analyzed it for a while. But then we spoke on the phone, and he casually mentioned he'd been staying at his girlfriend's. We hardly even knew each other, he said. I agreed.

And, really, I hardly even knew myself. My glasses weren't right; my future was uncertain; I was never *really* with the band. Seeing something that wasn't there seemed better than the other option at the time.

Marissa Walsh

Rose-Colored Glasses
(or, Things You Might Not Want to Overlook in a Roommate)

1. She has a cat and you are allergic.
2. She makes you pay half in cash and half in a money order made out to her landlord.
3. She won't let you use the kitchen, except to wash your pans in her sink.
4. She makes you clean the bathroom as much if not more than she does, even though her girlfriend is there all the time and you barely come out of your room to use the bathroom because you are afraid.
5. She does rituals before entering the park.

6. She doesn't work because of a carpal tunnel–related disability.

7. She will only rent to you if you are a lesbian, which you say you are, even though it's not technically true.

Marissa Walsh

Eye of the Storm

My first job in New York was as a waitress at Who's on First, a now-defunct natural-foods restaurant in Brooklyn on Seventh Avenue between First and Second Streets. I had never been a waitress before, but I was desperate. I hadn't heard back about the publishing job I had interviewed for that fall, and my substitute-teacher savings were quickly diminishing. For some reason the owner of Who's on First, Ahmed, hired me.

I was a horrible waitress. Maybe not as bad as the *Mad About You* waitress, but close. I couldn't remember anything; I couldn't multitask; I was too flustered to be chatty. People kept asking if I was from the Midwest.

Herb and Jean were my regulars. The day they came in and Herb said, "We'll have the usual" for the first time, I got a warm where-everyone-knows-your-name Norm-on-the-corner-bar-stool feeling. Two bowls of chili—one plain—and an order of cornbread with *two* apple butters. They were easy.

The cook was not. He had no patience with me and would spend my entire shift cursing under his breath, shaking his head and glaring. Here's my advice: Don't start waitressing for the first time during Ramadan. Especially if the cook is Egyptian.

Ramadan was one of the few holidays I wasn't aware of from college. So I had no idea. When I found out, it all made sense. Of course he was grouchy.

Our breakthrough came after a particularly bad night when every table had been full and high maintenance and I had almost walked out. At the end of my shift he handed me a plate with a fabulous-looking dessert on it. We didn't serve it at the restaurant, so I assumed he had made it for his evening feast. "Eat this," he grunted. A peace offering. It was delicious.

Waitressing is all about action. There's no time to think; you just do. It is not one of the GWG professions. And I didn't last long.

Wide-Angle Lens

If you are willing to work for free (I was, briefly) and you have a driver's license (I did), you can do almost anything in New York, like, for example, work in the production office of an indie film. My second job in New York entailed getting lunch every day for the entire office. Just be sure the two cranky guys (a.k.a. producers) receive theirs first or else they might go all Harvey on your ass. Indie? Right. Eventually I actually read the script for the film I was working on and saw that it sucked. The costume designer liked my, uh, "look" and took Polaroids of me every day—just my clothes, not my face— to base one of the character's wardrobes on mine. My look consisted of the glasses that were not me and definitely not New York, oversized overalls, and heavy Doc Marten–type shoes. I was unsure where the inspiration was coming from. I finally quit. I was not in the credits. But I was a bespectacled extra in one scene at the Rockefeller Center skating rink.

Love Is Blind

During my first summer in New York, my best friend from high school, Tricia, got married. She asked me to do a reading of my choice at the ceremony. I tried writing something, but nothing was working, so I decided to use the last four paragraphs of *Jazz* by Toni Morrison, which I had just finished reading. It was about love, and it had moved me, and it felt right. The obvious choice would have been *The Prophet* or First Corinthians. But I was a GWG. I needed to be different.

I wasn't wearing my glasses that day, but I should have played it safe. I should have had a backup plan, but I went with it, and not too far in I started bawling, and I couldn't stop. I tried to keep going, but no one could understand me, and I tried to make a joke, but I felt ridiculous. When I was done Trish gave me a hug, and back in the pew my date—who was my mother—whispered, "What was that all about?"

"Torn contact," I lied.

A job can be your . . . means of participating, instead of having your nose pressed up to the glass.

—Sex and the Single Girl,
HELEN GURLEY BROWN

The
If I Can Make It There
Pair

1996~1999

The Purchase

On my one-year anniversary of living in New York City, I finally found the perfect pair of glasses. In the "Best of New York" issue of *New York* magazine I had read about an eyeglass shop called MyOptics, which was full of the hippest designer frames I had ever seen—GWG heaven. The attentive salespeople actually wanted to help. They happily offered their opinions, and theirs were opinions I could trust. They let me try on every pair in the store, and then they all crowded around to see me in these. "They look hot," the guy in charge said. Sold.

After two months of waitressing and production-assisting, I had gotten the publishing job I had interviewed for in my suit the previous fall. It started out as a paid internship, but as of the new year had evolved into an editorial assistant position with full benefits. I could finally afford New York glasses.

I bought a pair of black Frye boots the same day.

For the first time ever, I had cool glasses. *Really* cool. And no one else seemed to have them; I felt unique. I received compliments. They were small and brown and cat's-eye, and they stood out. Maybe I was ready to stand out. New York was a place you could wear cat's-eye glasses. New York was a place *I* could wear cat's-eye glasses. New York was where the store clerks told you you looked hot.

I picked up my cat's-eyes—the coolest glasses I had ever known, the first pair I had bought myself, with my own money from my first real job, on my first credit card, and in New York—on Martin Luther King Day, with my friend Zoe. Leaving, I walked down the street and felt like I was seeing the world for the first time. Everything was crisp. Everything was in focus.

A View to a Kill

Not surprisingly, my first apartment in New York hadn't lasted long. I moved out and sublet with Rachel and Jen for a few months, then slept on Jessye's, Zoe's, and Kristine's couches, then moved in with an older alum of my college who rented out her two extra bedrooms. I was beginning to understand what they meant by "If I can make it there, I'll make it anywhere." GWGs aren't happy being nomads. They need a safe place to put their glasses while they sleep.

One day my friend Michelle, who was in a similar housing situation, called to tell me she had found a great apartment. A two-bedroom in Little Italy for $850. Her friend lived in the building, so she had gone to see it. It needed a lot of fixing up, but she thought it was worth it. There was one catch, though. (In New York there was always a catch.) The building was owned by the Mafia, and we had to pay our rent in cash. I moaned, but then said, "Well, at least it's a safe building," which seemed to be what a New Yorker would say—especially a New Yorker desperate for an apartment.

The apartment was above one of those tourist-trap Italian restaurants. There had been a mob hit at the restaurant across the street, someone told me. Everything would be fine as long as I paid my rent, I reminded myself. But what if I couldn't pay my rent? In cash, no less? The mob would suck my father dry just as the poor man was preparing for retirement. They'd ruin my mother's political career, and my brother Joseph would have a little "accident" one day at the skating rink. All because I couldn't find an apartment in New York City.

Michelle and I had to meet Giovanni, the building super, at the restaurant downstairs, where he was also the manager. He kept us waiting in the lounge, then handed us standard job-application forms to fill out. We lied about our salaries, but even with the lies he couldn't believe we lived on so little. *If he only knew,* I thought. I wanted to lie about more, but couldn't. Should I really give him my social-security number or my mother's maiden name? They had had a problem with the previous tenant and wanted to avoid such problems in the future, Giovanni explained. I nodded and smiled.

He didn't show us the apartment, but said he would

review our applications and call us. Two days later we got the call. Giovanni had passed our applications on to Bitsy, the woman he said was in charge. Michelle and I knew better. We'd seen the movies; Bitsy was not in charge. Nevertheless, we couldn't see the apartment until we saw Bitsy.

Bleached blond, with skin that was too tan for late September, Bitsy wore too much gold jewelry and looked like she wanted to pinch our cheeks. She looked us up and down, and nodded her head. "Okay, girls," she said.

Giovanni escorted us upstairs through a door in the restaurant that led directly into the stairwell of the building. I didn't like that access. On the way up to the apartment, he explained that the woman who had lived there before was not the kind of person they wanted living in the building. "She had lots of *visitors*, if you know what I mean," he said, and looked at me. I knew what he meant. I didn't like Giovanni.

And I didn't like the apartment. Michelle had warned me that the place needed work, so I had prepared for the worst, but it was even worse than that. It was a dump: small, no closets, a broken window, rotting floorboards, and no bathroom—just a toilet in a tiny closet and a shower in the kitchen. We could fix it up, Michelle said, and I wanted to agree, wanted to make it work, but then Giovanni told us the deal: They didn't fix anything, unless it was plumbing-related, and then he called one of his "people" to take care of it. Rent must be paid in cash. The phone and electric would be turned on when we moved in, and every month a bill would arrive, but it would be in someone else's name, with our apartment number on it. We weren't to worry about this; we were just to bring the bills to him, pay him in cash, and that's it. No questions.

I, of course, had too many questions. And no desire to lose my glasses and dark hair to the Witness Protection Program. I had seen enough. We didn't take the apartment.

If You See Her, Say Hello

High School Matt picked me up at my parents' house in Lynn. It could have been eleventh grade, but it was actually the day after Thanksgiving and we were both home from New York. "You Oughta Know" came on the radio, Matt cranked it, and we started singing along at the top of our lungs. "I am here to remind you . . ." Until we saw our friend's father getting out of his car in the funeral-home parking lot. Then we quickly turned the radio down and waited for him to go inside before we got out.

Yvette was the first person my age I knew who died. She was twenty-four and the only one of the four in the car who had been killed. It was a stupid death, the kind that makes people shake their heads and cluck. The kind that affects everyone, even people who didn't know her, because everyone agrees it just shouldn't happen that way, that young. She was engaged, the obituary said, and it made me sad that I hadn't known that, that I'd had to see it in the newspaper like everyone else. You lose touch with friends, but you assume you will see them again *someday*. You never think it's going to be permanent.

Hindsight Is 20/20

After a year and a half in New York I quit my publishing job and went to Martha's Vineyard for the summer to work for an older (read "elderly") couple. I had spent one cruel summer in New York without air-conditioning, and I wasn't looking forward to another one. Not sure I wanted to be an editor, I was ambivalent about my job. So when my friend mentioned that some friends of her parents were desperate for someone to help them out on the Vineyard over the summer—their first person had fallen through—and it included room and board, I said I was interested. It seemed like a financially viable way to get out of town for a few months and think about what to do next.

The Grandmother seemed sweet on the phone. My father suggested that perhaps I should meet her first. "There's no time," I told him. "They needed someone to start already." I gave two weeks' notice, sublet my room, and left town.

When I got off the ferry, I found a frail old woman with a shock of white hair. On the drive back to the house, I quickly discovered that I would have been safer driving without my glasses than with her behind the wheel. If I had met her first, as my father had suggested, I wouldn't have taken the job. Somehow my father always knew best.

I had gone from editorial assistant to "grandmother's helper." My new job description was to cook, clean, grocery shop, and do general tasks around the house. But that job title and description were way out-of-date. The woman was infirm, her grandchildren were grown, and I couldn't cook. I had been honest with her about it over the phone, but in her eagerness for someone—anyone—she had said that we would work it out together. My friend Jessye had sent me off with a fun cookbook of her own simple recipes. But The Grandmother preferred the way-out-of-my-league *Silver Palate*. I could make eggs, grilled cheese, and pasta; she wanted swordfish, mussels, and steak tartare. She wasn't really able to help. But she insisted on having people over for dinners and cocktail parties. It was not at all what I had expected.

Having never spent a summer on the Vineyard, it hadn't occurred to me that we would be having regular guests, and she hadn't mentioned it in our phone conversation. I set the table, served the meal, and sat and ate with her, her husband, and whatever unsuspecting guest happened to be dining with us that evening. Then I cleared and cleaned up. The faux-egalitarian setup made me—and some of the guests—uncomfortable. I would have preferred to be downstairs with my people, *Gosford Park* style. But The Grandmother and her husband were Cambridge Liberals. Most of our guests dealt with it by either ignoring me or trying too hard.

I caught a break in that The Grandmother was often invited *out* to dinner. One night she asked me to pick her up at a well-known cartoonist's house. She couldn't walk far, so she instructed me to drive right up onto his lawn when I came to pick her up, insisting he had said it was okay. So I did, and as I was turning around, the cartoonist came running outside (with a thought bubble that said, "What the &!$@ are you doing?!?" coming out of his mouth). I explained, and he calmed down and invited me in for dessert. All I had to do was mention The Grandmother's name anywhere and all was forgiven.

While The Grandmother was charming and sweet, The Husband was a curmudgeon. I cooked the eggs wrong; the mussels got cold. He seemed to complain about everything I did.

At one point during the summer we had mice. I had found the droppings in a drawer that held old phone books and lobster crackers, so the exterminator put traps in there. I got an anticipatory thrill every time I opened the drawer and was then disappointed to find nothing. The day I did find something, I was home alone, having just dropped The Grandmother off at a dinner. I thought about pretending I hadn't seen it until she returned. But it was my job to deal with it. So I did.

The next day, when I pulled the drawer out to clean it, some wriggly teeny-tiny pink barely-born mice fell to the ground. I screamed and ran away. The Grandmother and I stood there together, clutching each other, not sure what to do. The Husband finally came in to the kitchen to see what all the commotion was about. He made some disparaging remark, got the dustpan, swept them in, and walked out to the backyard.

I felt like the petulant girl in a Hallmark Hall of Fame television movie, sent against her will to stay with her grandparents for the summer so they could melt her cold heart and straighten her out with their tough love. Except that I was twenty-four, not related to these people, and being paid. I had left my cat's-eye confidence in New York. I was depressed and couldn't see a way out of the situation. I wanted to quit, but my parents strongly advised against it. It wouldn't be fair, they said. I knew they were right.

Toward the end of the summer, the husband of one of The Grandmother's friends pulled me aside and thanked me for everything I was doing for The Grandmother. He said he knew how hard it was, and that everyone appreciated it more than I knew. I looked at him incredulously and felt like the biggest asshole.

I loved The Grandmother. *She* wasn't the problem. She was an amazing, inspirational woman. A writer and a sharp wit, she knew everyone who was anyone on the island, and, more important, knew everything *about* everyone. Which she happily shared with me. She was always trying to get me to cut my hair, which had spent the summer in a ponytail. She insisted she could change my life by introducing me to her hairdresser. It had already worked for one person, she claimed. I would smile noncommittally and wonder when my glasses would come up in her makeover plans.

One night she had four cocktail parties to attend. Four. She was eighty. I chauffeured her from house to house, but she couldn't find the last one. It was back in the woods, and perhaps she had forgotten the way, but she kept telling me to try one turn and then another. But it was getting dark, and there were deer and no streetlights and I didn't want to get lost. The party was most certainly over. I put my foot down and drove home.

But that's the only time I ever stood up to her. Her kids wanted me to keep her from driving, which made me uncomfortable. So I just offered to bring her everywhere instead.

One day, I pulled up to the ramp right in front of the bank's door to let her out so she wouldn't have to walk from the parking lot. "Don't move," I said. "I'll be right back." But she didn't wait, and in the two minutes it took me to park she fell. Into a shrub. By the time I got there, she was scraped up and the bank people had called the ambulance. (Liability!) Her delicate skin had peeled away. She was so vulnerable, like an overturned turtle. I despaired all the way home about how I was going to explain it to The Husband, and felt so much like crying that I laughed instead.

Near the end of the summer, we were walking in the garden, her arm in mine, and The Grandmother said she had gotten emotionally attached. The Helper didn't know what to say. My eyes filled behind my New York cat's-eyes, but I knew it was time to go back.

Pictures of You

My actual grandmothers were very different. My Irish grandmother always seemed old. Probably because she was: I was 28 when she died at age 102. She wore flowered dresses and orthopedic shoes and, yes, cat's-eye glasses. They didn't seem cool at the time. She came over here on the boat when she was eighteen. In her passport photo, she is not smiling. She has clear skin, thick dark hair cut in a bob, and thick, black-framed glasses.

My Italian grandmother, on the other hand, always seemed young. She wears reading glasses to do her crosswords now, but she still goes to Atlantic City, and her hair has been the same honey color for years. I have a picture of her and my mother at Revere Beach with "1956" written on it in her handwriting. Her hair is up, with fashionable bangs. Her lips are slightly parted, in a half smile. She is thinking about something else.

Somehow, the pictures of my grandmothers both look remarkably like me.

I Saw Him Standing There

I was not planning on making out on the Peter Pan bus to Boston. But it was the third of July and I was heading up to my new job on Martha's Vineyard. Anything was possible. Which was why I hadn't been able to pack lightly. At Port Authority I actually paid a homeless guy to help carry my bags. He joked that I must have been transporting a dead body. I didn't deny it.

※ ※ ※

I had planned on sleeping with him when I returned to New York. Until I saw him again. Apparently I had forgotten what he looked like—or never knew—because as I descended the final set of stairs and saw him standing there in the tiny space between the two glass doors of my building, my stomach turned. It was not unlike the feeling I get when I discover a still-squirming mouse in a glue trap. My first impulse is to just pretend it's not there. But then I always end up putting it in a garbage bag.

I contemplated heading back upstairs (there was still a locked door between us, after all) but I didn't. He had come all the way from the Upper West Side. Which he reminded me of when I opened the door. He was heaving and dripping with sweat, and the book he was carrying was getting soggy. We did not kiss hello. "I was sorta hoping I could leave this upstairs." This, meaning his book. And I knew he was and I knew why he wanted to, so I held the outside door open for him and walked out. It would all be over in less than two hours. I could eat fast. He tried again. "It's pretty rude to expect me to come all the way out to Brooklyn and not even offer me a glass of water." What had I been thinking? It was a dark bus, I guess, and I do wear glasses.

"Oh. Well, I didn't want you to have to walk up four flights after coming all the way out to Brooklyn."

I walked fast down the sidewalk just to make him scurry to keep up with me. He was shorter than I was, and I didn't like it. He had seemed so much taller before. But we had been sitting down.

A nice foreign couple had asked if I wouldn't mind moving to another seat so they could sit together. Surprisingly, I hadn't minded. That's when the trouble started. I had seen him in line. "Hey, why don't you sit with me? Then you can watch my backpack while I go put this bag under the bus." So, shockingly, I did. Even though I hate it when people misjudge their luggage and then clog up the aisle lugging it back outside. But for some reason I didn't pull the girl-with-a-book thing this time. I just sat and waited for him to return. The thin but durable wall that exists between fellow travelers had already been scaled. He seemed harmless. Earnest. I was intrigued. And I had a long ride ahead of me.

Yes, I had in fact called him from the Vineyard during the mouse incident. I'd had no one else to call. Okay, I did have other people to call, but I wanted to call him. I wanted to call a boy. My boy, or at least someone who wanted to be. I wanted to be a girl. He was no help. He wasn't that kind of boy. He was busy writing. "Call the exterminator," he said. "I forgot chicks get bothered by stuff like that."

"Yeah," I said, "Me too."

He'd called me once, too. Called to thank me for all my free publishing advice. Said he wanted to repay me by taking me away for a romantic weekend somewhere when I got back to New York.

"If I could afford to take you to Paris I would, but I can't. So how about Montreal? I want to take you to Montreal."

"Maybe we should actually go on a date first. Or perhaps we could just meet on a plane somewhere, make out, and then go our separate ways."

"Please let me take you to Montreal."

"I've already been to Montreal. And I don't speak French.

I was tempted, though. It's not often a girl gets asked to go on an all-expenses-paid weekend vacation to Canada. Well, yeah, I guess some girls do.

We had decided on a pizza place under the Brooklyn Bridge because I had never been there. He had. He had also been to a Cajun restaurant in the neighborhood. "I go there with my friend Mary every time I come out here to visit her. She always tries to get me drunk." I knew I was supposed to ask him more about this, maybe even pretend to be jealous of this Mary person. So I said, "Gee, I've never heard of that place."

There was a line at the restaurant. This gave him time to tell me all about the book he was writing. He didn't have an agent yet. Some of the chapters had been published as short stories, and some important people had already agreed to give him blurbs.

"He sounds lonely," said my mother.

"He does?"

"Yes."

"But so am I!"

"That's because you're on an island with old people."

"Oh. But what if he's the love of my life?"

"He's not."

🥢 🥢 🥢

We were finally seated. The restaurant was quite warm from the brick oven; he was still sweating. Frank was on the wall and the jukebox. Fly *me* to the moon. I gave him the Heisman before our dinner even arrived.

"So, I've decided I just want to be friends."

"What? What are you talking about? The night is young. How could you possibly know that now?"

I knew.

"I just think it would be better to leave what happened on the bus on the bus. You know, like Vegas. I was hoping to avoid a misunderstanding later."

He tried again: "Why are you so tense? Why don't you just relax? Let's just see what happens."

GWGs hate when people tell them to relax.

I ordered a large pie with extra garlic, peppers, and onions. When the check came we went Dutch.

He insisted on walking home via the Promenade so that he could say, "This is the most romantic spot in Brooklyn and you're not going to let me hold your hand?" And I said, "No." So he said, "Don't think I'm leaving without a good-night kiss." And I said, "Well, you are." And he fumed and wouldn't look at me as we walked to the subway.

"Did you ever see that movie about the twentysomethings who meet on a train in Europe somewhere? I think Ethan Hawke was in it. They talk all night and fall in love. What was it called?" I knew the movie he was referring to, but I didn't want him to know that I had also been reminded of it. Finally he remembered. "*Before Sunrise*?" And I knew that he had known all along too. "I've never seen it," I lied.

But I did go along when he took my hand. And even though we hadn't started the trip as costars, I went for it when he leaned in for the staged kiss. Took him by surprise. And then I was the leading lady.

My mother had come inside the station to wait so she could help me with my stuff. He'd insisted on carrying my bag off the bus, but I don't think I introduced him to her. Peter Pan names all their buses. Ours was called Tunnel of Love.

I saw him on the subway once. I switched cars.

Double Vision

The cat's-eye frames came with nine lives. That fall I landed on my feet back in New York. One Sunday afternoon I was registering voters for the '96 presidential election in front of the Key Food on Seventh Avenue in Park Slope when I saw them. My glasses. On someone else. The woman wearing them stopped and exclaimed. We did the requisite "Where did you get them? How long have you had them? Have you ever seen anyone else with them?" Not until that day. Apparently Gotham was big enough for more than one Catwoman.

Myopia

The only Christmas Eve I ever worked was not in retail or emergency-room medicine or law enforcement, but in publishing. When I returned from the Vineyard, I had gotten another publishing job and somehow the two of us from Boston Catholic families were in the office until three p.m. on Christmas Eve, because the boss was convinced that something would happen. Nothing happens in publishing for about two weeks around the holidays, and everyone knows it. But I had only been there a few months, so I didn't feel I could complain. Plus, I was part-time, and since the office was technically open, if I didn't come in I wouldn't get paid. (Happy holidays!) Also, I was terrified of the boss. I had been screamed at already, for writing a phone number down incorrectly. (I was vindicated when the author called back and apologized for having left the wrong number.)

My coworker and I had made a plan to take the shuttle up to Boston together, so I didn't think it would be so bad. But when I got to the airport and took my backpack off to get my wallet out, the outside pocket was unzipped and my wallet wasn't there. It must have been stolen on the subway on the way to the airport. It was my own fault for leaving it in the outer pocket and keeping my backpack on my back in a crowded subway car the day before Christmas.

If I had been alone, I would have been stuck at the airport. But my colleague kindly put both tickets on her credit card. My brother picked me up in Boston and we drove straight to my aunt's for our annual Christmas visit. I spent the first hour of it reporting my credit cards stolen.

I lasted another year in the job, but my cat's-eye lives were down to seven.

Cat's-Eyes by the Numbers

Number of cities visited: 6

Number of apartments lived in: 3

Number of close friends who left New York for San Francisco: 3

Number of jobs quit: 2

Number of temp jobs in the Chrysler Building involving a walkie-talkie: 1

Number of guys who meowed at me on the street: 1

Hide and Seek

I was on the subway, reading, when I heard, "Okay, this is a stickup. Everyone put all your money on the floor." My heart skipped a beat. I looked up. The man who had spoken was holding a banana in the air. I adjusted my cat's-eyes and went back to my book.

GEORGE: *"What kind of a sick, demented person wants another person's glasses?"*
ELAINE: *"Yeah, especially those frames."*

—*Seinfeld*

The

Men _Often_ Make Passes

at Girls Who Wear Glasses

Pair

1999~2002

The Purchase

I still didn't know what I wanted to do with my life, but I had been temping without health insurance for long enough. I was tired of the uncertainty. And the debt. When a fellow GWG offered me another publishing job with great benefits, I took it, thinking I would be there for six months to a year, just long enough to figure things out. I stayed for almost seven years.

It had been many years since my last eye exam, so now that I had health insurance, I made an appointment.

An eye appointment when you have finally found the perfect pair of frames is risky business; it leaves you open to the possibility of a prescription change. A prescription change usually means a frame change. This is what happened to me.

Of course, I didn't *have* to get new frames. I could always have kept the old frames and just changed the lenses. Or bought a new pair of the same model. But I decided I was too young to pull a Carrie Donovan or a Lew Wasserman. The cat's-eye frames were so dirty and old and faded from three years of daily wear that I figured it was time for a change. I had a new job. I wanted to start fresh.

I left my ophthalmologist's office with my prescription and headed to MyOptics again, eager to repeat my earlier success.

But it wasn't the same. My friend Emily came to help, but I didn't know how to replicate the magic of my previous pair.

My new frames were larger and squarer, less catty. I was happy with them at the time. But deep down I couldn't help feeling that I would never be able to find anything better than I already had.

At the time I lived in The Vanderbilt, my fourth New York City address but my first, and in some ways only, home. I had lived there with Anderson, a fellow GWG and one of my closest friends from college, for three years. We called our apartment The Vanderbilt because it was on Vanderbilt Avenue. Of course.

Our timing had been perfect. We were both looking for the same thing in a living situation. And being roommates made us even better friends. We hosted roof parties and New Year's parties and Ides of March parties and had a weekly "family night" where we watched *Buffy the*

Vampire Slayer and ate dinner together. People slept on our couch. We had a roof garden. But then Anderson fell in love—with Mika, a friend of mine, actually—and it was time to grow up. Our twenties were officially over. The pretend-sitcom we liked to consider life at The Vanderbilt had been cancelled.

I was in denial for a long time about things changing. It felt like a breakup. I halfheartedly searched for a new roommate, knowing that, like with my glasses, I would never be able to find a better model of what I already had, but unable to see that it was time for me to move on too. I finally settled for someone at the last minute, right before rent was due. But there was no replacing Anderson. My spin-off, like *Joey*, was a big failure.

Ocular

Getting ones eyes examined is an intimate, even erotic, experience. The room is dark, first of all, which sets the scene. Then my ophthalmologist (that word!) tells me to look into his eyes. He touches my chin and tilts my head toward him. He rests his palm on my cheek to pass an instrument back and forth in front of each eye. Our breathing is the only sound in the room. His face is just inches away from mine. Then a switch is hit, the lights return, the stuffed animals above the light box at the end of the room are visible, and we talk about the Boston Marathon.

Eye of the Tiger

I had a new job and a new pair of glasses; I was ready for Beginner Lindy Hop. My friend Ace was ready, too. We weren't sure where it would lead. Maybe some digits. Maybe some dance dates. Maybe he would start wearing one of those wallet chains. At the very least we hoped we would be able to wow our friends at the next party.

The first night our Italian instructor, Paolo, put on some Ella and instructed us to warm up. "Just bounce," he said. He was wearing a cap slightly cocked to one side, like his smile, and he reminded me of Eric from the first *Real World*. You know, the shirtless guy who went on to host *The Grind*. So we were bouncing, and some people were snapping and getting down, and I looked at Ace and we burst out laughing. It was weird. I hadn't been in dance class since I was a kid taking ballet, and that had not been coed. This had a distinctly eighth-grade-dance feel to it. I already felt taller than all the men in the room. I looked at Ace again, and we couldn't stop laughing, and I was afraid we were going to get kicked out. It wasn't funny. Everyone else was bouncing. They were all in control.

By the time the actual dancing began, I had calmed down. There were about thirty people in our class, equal parts men and women, so everyone had a partner. Ace and I started the step as a pair. I was perfectly happy dancing with him, once I got used to his hand (any hand) on the small of my back. It had been a while since I had been touched.

Things were going well until we had to "rotate." Perhaps *this* is where someone got the idea for speed dating. Paolo would shout "Rotate!" and the men would move one person forward. The requisite introductions would take place, or wouldn't, depending. And then I would adapt to the man who was shorter than I was, the man who gripped too hard, the man who sweated too much, the man who felt around. Waltzing with Uncle Frannie at family weddings had never been so intimate. I tried not to cling to Ace or make it seem as if we were a couple. I didn't want to neglect my duties as a wingwoman. But I did not want to rotate! Really, I was content with him. He was only a friend, and that was all I wanted, but he was the perfect dance partner.

Paolo would always pick someone from the class to

help him demonstrate the next move. He never picked me. I was taller than he, weighed a little more than I should have, and never quite wore the right dancing outfit or shoes. The only guy I had my eye on, a guy in a suit and glasses, exchanged numbers with a woman at the last class. One of Paolo's partners.

Ultimately, though, that didn't matter. Swing class had strengthened my friendship with Ace, and it had been fun. It got me moving—literally and figuratively. I was back in the swing of things, starting to change the way I viewed myself. It was only the beginning.

In Plain Sight

There's an old *New Yorker* cartoon that pretty much sums up dating for the GWG. A woman standing on the front stoop of a brownstone says to a man standing down on the sidewalk, "I'd invite you in, but I'm sort of a mess right now."

I felt that way for a long time. But then 1998 turned into 1999. On New Year's Eve, Anderson had Prince's "1999" queued up on the stereo. She hit play just after midnight, as soon as the fireworks had ended and the hundred or so guests at our New Year's Eve party were coming down from the roof. "1999" segued into "Little Red Corvette." It was one of those transcendent moments. The crowd danced as one. The floor bounced. Everyone was there. I was happy.

I went to bed alone.

When I woke up too early the next morning, my friend Matt was sleeping on our couch, fully dressed. He quickly hopped up, grabbed a broom, and helped me put the apartment back together. It was the best party he had ever been to.

I had met Matt three years before, at our mutual friend Sasha's party. He was wearing a bow tie and cool glasses, and he also worked in publishing. I didn't know anyone at the party, and I ended up spending most of the time talking to him.

We went on a few dates but I was sort of a mess then.

A few months after the New Year's party, we tried dating again. This time, however, I invited him in, and he waited on the couch while I shoved everything on my bedroom floor into the closet. GWGs often make passes at boys who wear glasses.

Guidelines for Kissing with Glasses

1. It is not necessary to remove your glasses before you kiss. You will harm neither yourself nor your partner.

2. Two bespectacled people can kiss comfortably. It's all about depth perception.

3. Don't take your glasses off too soon in the relationship. Once they are off, you are truly naked, and there is no going back.

4. If it gets to that point, decide if and when you want your partner to take them off for you.

5. Remember, without glasses, your eyes are visible. Your soul is on display. Alternative protection might be necessary.

I'll Be Your Mirror

I didn't want to pull a Yoko, but I had never seen Matt play drums before. So I went with him to a practice space with drums and amps on the Lower East Side to watch. It was fucking freezing, and we were a bit late. The space was in a diminishing part of the Lower East Side that had yet to be gentrified. It was the only reason to go there.

He and John, collectively known as the Plummers, had been in bands together in college, but now it was just the two of them. John sang, played rhythm guitar, and wrote songs. Matt drummed like Keith Moon. They needed a bass player but hadn't advertised or done anything about it. Matt's drums were still in his parents' garage in Pittsburgh.

The time slots at practice spaces are like therapy time slots. There is always some overlap, and you end up awkwardly having to say hello to the person coming after you.

The band in our room had taken advantage of our tardiness, and they had to pack up hastily while we stood there waiting.

The place was called Tasty Fish, but it was not tasty. It was moldy. It was punk. We went down rickety wooden stairs to the basement practice room. The stairs were not permanent. They could be pulled up, like the stairs to an attic or a bunk-bed ladder. I guess if the neighbors complained, they could have just boarded over the whole basement when the cops came. But there were no neighbors.

And my visit to the bathroom confirmed that there weren't many women, either.

I closed the door to the room when the other band left. I wanted to make sure we could get out again, since it was the type of door that looks like you can't. It was like you were locked in from the outside. And you couldn't hear anything once the music started. And there were no windows. Matt said, "You're gonna need these," and stuffed some tissues in my ears. I perched on the edge of a cruddy sofa in the corner of the room. It was cleaner than the floor, but not by much. The stuffing was coming out, and it had stains that made you look twice. I perched, and they started playing, and I pulled out a book. It felt weird to sit there, reading. They played as if I weren't there, and I felt shy about even looking at them. I would steal a glance and then feel guilty, because they were not self-conscious at all.

It made me smile—smirk, almost. I shouldn't have been there, observing. It was too intimate. They were boys, playing, and I had been allowed in their locker room.

We all drank Rolling Rock and said "rock and roll" a lot. Matt took his shirt off. He plays hard, so hard that he sweats. At some point something on the ground near my foot caught my eye. It was a bloody Band-Aid. Someone had bled for his art. Someone had blisters on his fingers. That's what it was all about, right? Sweat. And blood. I made sure my shoe didn't touch it.

When it was time to leave, John said, "If you're gonna be our groupie, then you're gonna have to carry the beer." He'd teach me how to play if I bought a bass, he said. And Matt said, "She's a really good singer," and I said, "Yeah, I could sing backup or something," and John said something about Nico.

A few days later I put the Stones on the turntable and practiced singing with a British accent. A Pez dispenser was my microphone, and I sang "Under My Thumb" and changed the pronouns. Hours later I was getting hoarse and keeping one ear out for Anderson on the stairs. I didn't want her to see me pretending to be a rock star—at twenty-seven a bit late, but just like everybody else.

Close Your Eyes

As a GWG, sleeping with someone makes you vulnerable in different ways. There's the obvious emotional vulnerability that happens if you care about the person. There's the physical vulnerability of your naked face on display up close, which could be viewed as an invitation to comment on the difference in your appearance: "Wow, your face is so much softer without your glasses." And finally there's the fact that when you take off your glasses, you are blind. What if you don't know the person that well, and they are some kind of joker, and they hide your glasses? Or what if they don't have a proper bedside table on which to place your glasses so they are within arm's reach? Where are you supposed to put them? On the floor? I need to see until the minute I turn out the light. In fact I keep my glasses on until after I turn out the light, so I can adjust to the darkness with vision. Then I remove them and put them on my night table, right next to the phone.

Out of Sight, Out of Mind

When we see something out of the ordinary, the first thing we do is want someone else to see it, too. We know they've got to see it with their own eyes to believe it. We also want confirmation that we're not crazy.

Uh, Marissa?" I looked up from taking my keys out of the door. We had been out drinking. Matt was stopped in his tracks.

"There's a bird in the apartment."

I slowly took in the scene. One of the living room window screens was lying on the floor. And yes, there was a pigeon happily nesting on the blinds above the window. I was sure my new roommate was involved.

The living room had three windows, all facing the street. The one on the left was in the little alcove that my new roommate used as her "studio." There was no screen on this window. The other two windows were in the living room proper, and they both had screens. It's not difficult to deduce how the bird got in. The screens were not ripped in any way. There was no evidence of forced entry. I'm sure it walked right on in her open window. But it didn't matter how it got in (or who was to blame). What mattered was how to get it out.

My new roommate's bedroom door flew open. She stuck her head out, and it became apparent to me that her boyfriend was in there with her. "Hey, guys, there's a bird in the apartment," she said, and then closed the door again. I walked toward her door in disbelief, thinking she was just throwing on her robe and would reemerge in a second to come explain, but she never did. She had, however, also left a note outside my bedroom door. "Warning!" it read. "There is a bird in the apartment!" No shit, Hitchcock.

Matt asked for a broom, and I handed one to him, then hovered in the hallway with the apartment door open. I wanted to be able to close the door, in case the bird attacked, but I also didn't want to miss the action. And I wanted to offer Matt moral support, of course. It was my apartment, after all.

The thing is, a bird used to live in the apartment. Anderson's bird, Woodstock. But he was a cockatiel, and he lived in a cage. Every so often he would say, "Hello, pretty bird," if my former roommate waved a paper-towel tube at him. Sometimes he sang. The bird nesting above my window was no Woodstock. It was a pigeon. A flying rat.

Matt had opened all of the living room windows and was stealthily attempting to corner the pigeon with the broom. I got the phone and called my father. My father grew up in a city. I've never seen him mow the lawn. But he has a quality that makes him seem like an authority on mice, flying cockroaches, hissing radiators, and ants. He's a lobbyist. He was half-asleep. "Get a towel!" he shouted. "Right!" I said. *This* is why I call him in emergencies. Why had I forgotten about the towel? I had seen Anderson use a towel to get Woodstock in and out of the cage. I found a dirty towel and gave it to Matt.

But he didn't want to get close enough to use the towel. He was trying to get the pigeon to fly straight out the window. Unfortunately, the pigeon didn't want to do this. Matt swatted it with the broom, and it began to fly toward me. I screamed and ran out into the hallway. Why are we afraid of birds? Is it because a bird can land on your head? Or, for the non-GWG, poke out your eyes?

My roommate, in the meantime, had not made another peep. So I was being as loud as possible. How do you go to bed knowing there is a pigeon in your apartment? And why would you leave the screen off the window? Did she not make the connection that if one got in that way, others could too? I could understand if she was alone and didn't know what to do and waited up for us to come home so that we could all tackle the problem together. But knowing that her boyfriend, who had completed a mandatory stint in the Turkish army, was asleep in bed while my boyfriend, a mere civilian, was chasing a pigeon around with a broom pissed me off.

My father was still on the line, but he was not listening to my rant. Instead he interrupted me to ask, "Is Matt spending the night?"

Matt's final swing did the trick. The pigeon flew into the mantle, knocked over a pot, shat, then went out the window. Matt ran to close the window after it and brushed his hands off, like in the movies. I thanked my father and hung up.

I saw my roommate a few days later. "That was really weird about the pigeon," I said with a fake laugh. "I'm not sure how you expected to get it out of the apartment."

"Oh," she said, "we figured we would just leave the window open so it could fly out during the night."

My Italian grandmother is superstitious about birds. A bird in the house is bad luck, she says. If she receives a Christmas card with a bird on it, she will immediately turn it facedown so she doesn't have to look at it. I'm not entirely sure why she feels this way, but as I cleaned up the pigeon shit, I could sort of understand.

Foresight

I think I was actually the one, at a Brooklyn roof party, to point out the window across the way, in which some unwise couple was foreplaying with the lights on and the shades up. I didn't say anything at first, but the minute I did, everyone gathered around to watch. Soon we were a bunch of cackling, curious girls wondering too loudly, "Where is her head? What is he doing? What's taking so long?" Until finallyfinallyfinally the man stood up and pulled the blinds down.

Photo Montage

On 9/11, Times Square was full of people who couldn't get home and who, like me, didn't want to be inside their tall office buildings. They were looking up at the Jumbo-Trons, at the sky. A crowd ran toward me on Forty-second Street, screaming. I ran in the opposite direction without waiting to find out why. I walked downtown, against the flow, and it felt wrong. A grocery store had locked its doors, and customers were lined up outside, waiting to buy bottled water and toilet paper and canned soup. (Like that would help.) I actually wondered, as I walked home across the Fifty-ninth Street Bridge, if I would see anyone jump.

Watching too much TV, it was easy to convince myself that it was happening somewhere else. But when I went outside, I could smell it. At a back-to-school theme party a week and a half later the photocopied yearbook-picture decorations looked like the missing-person signs still hung up all over the city.

Now it's like when someone is gone and you realize you can no longer call up their face. It's faded; you need a photograph. I can't even visualize where in the skyline those buildings stood. I just assumed I'd always be able to look.

The Vision Plan Pair

2002 ~ 2003

Everybody seemed to be finding a partner and moving onto the floor—everybody except her. . . . She would end up being danced with by Mr Fanope, out of charity, and everybody would know that nobody had asked her. It's my glasses, she told herself. It's my glasses . . .

—MMA MAKUTSI, *In the Company of Cheerful Ladies,*
ALEXANDER McCALL SMITH

The Purchase

Sometimes a GWG finds herself in a situation with a limited budget. Frames can be expensive, after all, and if you're lucky enough to have a job that offers vision coverage, you need to use it.

My vision plan had assigned me to an office in the Diamond District, which is an odd place to be thinking about eyewear. (Unless it's a jeweler's monocle.) I knew immediately when I walked in that it was going to be hard to find an acceptable pair here. It was one of those one-stop shopping deals where you could both get your eyes examined and buy frames. I didn't approve. Examining eyes and choosing frames were two different—separate—activities. In fact, even though he was out of network, I had gone to my old ophthalmologist up in Massachusetts for my eye exam. I figured I would cut costs with the frames and lenses. I liked that he had my records and knew my eyes, and I wasn't ready to leave him yet.

Unlike my committed contact lens–wearing brother, Steven, who had stopped going to him years ago, I was loyal.

You always get what you pay for. The selection of frames could best be described as limited. I was only on Forty-seventh Street, but I was a world away from the GWG selection found downtown at MyOptics. But I was determined not to let my vision coverage go to waste. New York had brought out the pragmatist in me. I was still at the job I had thought would be a one-year thing. After Matt moved to Connecticut for grad school, I had taken over his eleven-by-eleven studio apartment between the Amtrak tracks and the Triborough Bridge in Queens (but had to keep dodging the landlord, who didn't know I lived there). In my mid-twenties I had pulled the credit card out for glasses, g&t's, and groceries, but I was older and wiser now. And out of credit-card debt. I didn't want to go back.

One day someone I worked with said, "Your face is too skinny for your glasses! You should get new glasses now that you've lost weight." This was not an unusual thing for her to say. And I did keep her comment in mind as I picked out the new frames. But when I went into her office to show her, she just said, "You should have taken me with you."

Matt had come with me. I'd picked the only frames in the store that worked: brown oval Donna Karans, even though they were a little extra on top of the insurance. Like my job and my apartment, they would do for now.

Standardized Snellen Acuity Chart

I hate this part of the eye exam. Sometimes I simply cannot see *any* difference between A and B. I am supposed to tell the doctor which is clearer—which I can see better—but I don't know. I could make an argument for each one. I always need to go back and look at the first one again. I forget. A had its strengths, maybe it was slightly crisper, but B allows me to see the bottom row, which is important, too. I don't feel qualified. Why is it up to me? Shouldn't he get a say? What if I choose wrong? I've tried to solve this problem by answering like this: "A?" or "B, I think, was *slightly* better," or "A, sort of. Can I see it again?"

Oh, Say Can You See

I don't want to take full credit, but my younger brother Joseph's decision to take ice-skating lessons may have been my influence. Growing up in the eighties, I was one of those girls who would watch the Olympics and decide I was going to be the next Mary Lou Retton. Or Rosalyn Sumners. Or Mary Decker. Or Kitty and Peter Carruthers. The sport didn't matter. I was all about the Wheaties box, the hug from Bela, the bouquet of roses, and the tears on the gold-medal stand as the national anthem played. The only problem was, my one attempt at skating lessons had ended rather abruptly when I discovered, to my dismay, that it wasn't as easy as it looked. And the uneven bars? Not recommended for a GWG.

When Joseph made it to the national skating championships as a novice, I started planning for the Olympics. I assumed we'd paint our faces red, white, and blue and sit in the stands chanting "U-S-A! U-S-A!" and waving little American flags. After Joe's program, the camera would flash to us with the caption "Joseph Walsh's family," and I'd be interviewed for the "Up Close and Personal" profile—"I'm the one who encouraged Joseph to skate!"—and during the medal ceremony we'd all cry.

But Joseph came in last.

He stopped skating competitively and took a job with Disney's *Anastasia on Ice* tour. I thought he was too talented to give up on the Olympics. There was always ice dancing, I told him. Look at Torvill and Dean! But he had made his decision.

Conveniently, the *Anastasia* tour came to Boston that Christmas, so my parents bought the entire family tickets. We couldn't wait to see Joseph. He would be playing the role of Vladimir for our show. But this was a Disney production, so being Vladimir consisted of wearing a costume, including a head, which made Joseph essentially unidentifiable. It could have been anyone under that head and we never would have known the difference. My parents had failed to mention this.

At Vladimir's first appearance my mother shouted, "There he is! That's Joe!" There was a pause as we leaned forward and squinted and tried to figure out where exactly Joe was. "In the costume!" my mother yelled, and we all laughed and cheered and chanted "Joe!" much to the confusion of other audience members.

After the show, we waited in the lobby, and when Joe emerged, we cheered again. He was not wearing the costume but his face was red and sweaty and smiling—it had definitely been him under there. And I realized, as our little cousins surrounded him for pictures and autographs, that he was happy. The Olympics had been *my* dream, from when I still dreamed in 20/20.

Invisibility Cloak

When I am not wearing my glasses, it seems possible that I could be invisible. I can't see you, so maybe—hopefully—you can't see me. Sometimes, when I take my glasses off to clean them and I am talking or listening to someone I can no longer see, it is as if my brain stops. I try to nod and make eye contact but my normal facial expressions feel exaggerated. I am suddenly Jerry Lewis in *The Nutty Professor*. Once I replace my glasses, I return to Dean Martin normal.

Sometimes I'll get on an elevator with someone I know or may have met before, and I'll hide in plain sight. I'll convince myself that I'm invisible. Or that they've forgotten they met me. I fail to remember that my glasses actually stand out. I'll forget that just because I can't see doesn't mean I can't be seen.

Focal Points

I prefer eye doctors with glasses.

My glasses do not look good on you so don't take them off me and try them on.

Yes, I do have a strong prescription.

Yes, I know I am not wearing my glasses today.

Eventually he—or she—will see you with your glasses on.

Beauty does not equal 20/20 vision.

Cold air + bar = foggy glasses. (Every time.)

I do not remember there being four girls with glasses in my fifth-grade class picture.

It is really not necessary to remove your glasses to be photographed.

I have never lost or broken a pair of glasses

I get mad at people who slow down to look at a wreck but I do it, too.

I still cover my eyes at the movies and remove my hands only when told it is safe.

I Can See for Miles

Even now, I have to remind myself: nearsighted means you can't see things far away, and farsighted means you can't see things close up. It has never felt right. Since what we *can't* see is more important, shouldn't it be the opposite?

I started out nearsighted. Now I am no-sighted.

Bear in mind that better eyesight—our most valuable possession—is possible to anyone with fair vision. The little time spent daily in improvement and care of the eyes is good insurance against the discomfort, inconvenience, and emotional despair of failing vision.

—How to Improve Your Sight,
MARGARET DARST CORBETT

The Jackie O Pair

2004-Present

The Purchase

My first pair of prescription sunglasses ever are Jackie O not Nicole Richie big, and when I wear them I like to pretend that people are looking at me, trying to figure out who I am.

Sunglasses used to be about hiding, about creating a barrier between you and the world. But now they have become so synonymous with celebrity that they, like a town car with tinted windows, do the opposite and attract attention. Sunglasses make you look more, because you assume there must be *someone* under there.

They also infuse instant glamour into any situation. When I wear sunglasses, I automatically feel like wrapping a scarf around my head and driving in a convertible. Not that I've ever actually done that, but with sunglasses it feels possible.

Indeed, the rules for regular glasses don't apply. People

wear all kinds of wacky sunglasses that they would never be able to pull off as glasses. Sadly, the options for GWGs are much less cool. The snap-on sunglass component? Lenses that darken automatically in sunlight? I don't think so.

I love sunglasses, but oddly, it had never occurred to me to get a prescription pair. So I could only wear them when I wore contacts, which was one of my motivations for keeping a pair of contacts around. But I haven't had contacts in years, and I missed wearing sunglasses. It was time.

I went back to my vision plan–approved place and once again found only one pair that worked for me: Ralph Lauren, which wouldn't be right for my regular glasses (or clothing). But for sunglasses they're fine. Of course, as long as they're dark enough, it's hard to go too wrong.

I often forget to bring them with me. And I have yet to master the glasses juggling of non-car-based errands-running and shopping. I feel self-conscious when I keep them on for too long inside. I want to explain to shop clerks that I am not Jack Nicholson and I am not trying to be; I'm just leaving my sunglasses on so I can see and because it's too much trouble to switch back to my regular glasses for only a few minutes. One day, like Whoopi Goldberg, I simply won't care.

Blinded by the Light

A few years ago, I was having my eyes examined, and my doctor asked if he could dilate my pupils. I said sure, since I wasn't driving, but I didn't really want him to. The drops always make me nervous, since it's the only time I can't see even with my glasses on. And what if, for some reason, I were unable to regain my focus? As I sat there in the waiting room trying to squint my eyes enough to read so I wouldn't freak out (not recommended), an elderly woman next to me struck up a conversation. I was happy for the distraction.

When it was time to leave, I took one step outside and immediately ducked back into the office for relief. The outside light was too strong—it hurt to open my eyes. This had never happened before. I asked the receptionist what to do. She handed me a rolled-up piece of black plastic and instructed me to place it between my glasses and my face. I was so grateful for the relief, I didn't even care that I looked like an idiot. Or that the black plastic was cutting into my face.

As I was leaving for the second time, I encountered the old woman. She, too, was wearing one of the black plastic strips, and we made small talk as I followed her, the blind leading the blind, to the subway. No one offered us a seat. Poor Stevie Wonder.

Corrective Lenses

I don't own a car. I only drive when I am at my parents' house in Massachusetts. In fact, I still have a Massachusetts driver's license. But that doesn't help me there. As a GWG, I have certain driving challenges, which are only exacerbated by the combination of large construction project and bad driving that is Boston. Whenever I return, a different piece of the expressway is underground. But there's never any warning, and all the Massholes are zipping past you like it's always been that way. I'm driving along outside, wearing my prescription sunglasses, when I will suddenly enter a tunnel, emerge briefly, then be plunged under again. If there is a passenger in the car, this is how it happens:

"Shit! We're going into a tunnel. Glasses! Glasses!" The passenger hands over the glasses, already opened, and takes the sunglasses, while the driver slides the glasses on in one swift motion. A few minutes later, outside: "The glare! The glare! Sunglasses! Sunglasses!" The passenger reverses the process. Only to repeat it again a few minutes later. It's helpful if the passenger has already been trained in this procedure.

If the GWG driver is alone, she will try to make it through the tunnel while wearing the sunglasses. Halfway through, she will freak out about how long the tunnel is and the fluorescent lights and she will feel like her eyesight is failing her. She will decide that the only way to make it safely is to switch to her glasses herself. For a split second she will be blind.

Marissa Walsh

Blind Spot

"Which would you rather be—blind or deaf?" was the question I was asked one day when I walked into work. An innocent enough question. "Deaf," I answered, without missing a beat. The music lovers argued with me, but I knew I was right. As the discussion wore on, one of my coworkers and I even admitted to an unwillingness to help blind people on the subway or across the street. I wasn't a very good Girl Scout.

A few days later I began to notice them. Suddenly, it seemed, I was running into white canes and seeing-eye dogs everywhere.

The Girl with Glasses Pair

2003 — Present

But I had my eyes closed. I thought I'd keep them that way for a little longer. I thought it was something I ought to do.

"Well?" he said. "Are you looking?"

—"Cathedral," RAYMOND CARVER

The Purchase

Life is too short to wear the wrong pair of glasses. I had wanted these blue vintage cat's-eye glasses with sparkly rhinestones for a long time, but I hadn't been ready. Until I found this pair at Fabulous Fanny's, a store that specializes in vintage frames. They were too good to pass up.

I still had my vision plan, but I was unhappy with my practical glasses and my practical life. I decided it was worth it to spend money on something I wore every day, something that was, in some ways, a part of me.

My eye exam was covered, but the optometrist seemed miffed that I had brought my own frames and wouldn't be buying any. He warned me that I was putting lenses in at my own risk. Because the frames were vintage, he would not be liable if anything happened to them.

I first wore them, not coincidentally, on a work trip to Germany. The trip was a big deal—my first time there, and my first time flying after a long hiatus. Germany seemed like the perfect place to break them in; everyone has cool glasses there.

I was still self-conscious. I thought I was making a big statement with my bold blue eyewear, but nobody blinked an eye. When there is something new or different about us, we're so aware of it that we assume others are too. But years later people I worked with—friends—asked me if I had gotten new glasses. They hadn't even noticed.

Some days I think my glasses are the only cool thing about me. Working for The Man, I sometimes found myself wearing clothes I would never be caught dead in otherwise. But I didn't purge these things from my closet. I just hoped the glasses would speak for themselves.

Wearing these glasses, I moved out of the tiny studio that had been Matt's and into my own big, sunny, one-bedroom apartment. I realized that life was also too short for the wrong job, and I quit. Almost two years after getting these glasses, but I did, and now my life is more in tune with my eyewear.

I was meeting a friend at her office for lunch and the receptionist said, "I love your glasses. I wish I was brave enough to wear them."

I smiled. "It took me a while."

And I'm not done. I actually need a new pair. The Girl-with-Glasses Pair is a work in progress.

Marissa Walsh

Sunglasses at Night

There comes a time in every GWG's life when she is ready to differentiate herself. You will know it when it happens. You will decide on a signature cocktail and accessory, which doesn't have to be your glasses. You will speak in exclamation points and use words like "divine" and "delightful." You will make pronouncements like, "One must always have leopard." You will embrace your inner Carrie Donovan and be happier for it.

How to Wear 'Em

Like you mean it.

Like you're ready to take them off.

Like you have 20/20 vision.

Like you can see through everyone in the room.

Like you want to be remembered.

Boy with Glasses

Random people on the street are always stopping Matt to tell him how much they love his glasses. "Where did you get them?" they run after him to ask. Then, if I am with him, they might look at me, realize I also have glasses, and add, "Oh, you have cool glasses too. Wow, you both have cool glasses." But I notice that he always gets it first. I am an afterthought, because the person doesn't want me to feel left out. If he didn't have distinctive glasses, would mine get all the glory? Or not even the second glance?

Second Pair of Eyes

I've been pretty lucky in my optic history; I've only had one glasses emergency. And it didn't involve broken glass. I fell asleep reading, and during the night I must have taken my glasses off, but in the morning they were gone. I looked (groped, really) everywhere but couldn't find them. There was no way to get help for this situation. I couldn't find the phone; I couldn't find my old pair; I couldn't see. I had fallen and I couldn't get up. I got down on my hands and knees and felt all around the bed, then under the bed, trying to keep myself calm. This is why people pair off, I thought, for these emergencies. Then, finally, there they were, in that under-the-bed place that is just out of reach.

I Can See Clearly Now

Because I didn't need new frames and my vision plan covered it, I got two pairs of contacts (one free!) from my optometrist at my last eye exam. He had to fit them, so I wore them home. I felt dizzy and naked. I haven't worn them since.

The spectacles were in Meg's hand. She put them carefully into the breast pocket of her blazer, and the knowledge that they were there somehow made her a little less afraid.

—*A Wrinkle in Time*, MADELEINE L'ENGLE

Four-eyed Guide

Glasses Rule

Great Girl-with-Glasses Moments

Four-eyed Guide

Album: *Girls with Glasses*, Partyline, www.partylinedc.com

Best Style Frame for Your Face Consultation:
www.eyeglass.com

Boys with Glasses: Woody Allen (pre-Soon-Yi), Elvis
Costello, Rivers Cuomo, David Letterman

Designer Frames: www.laeyeworks.com,
www.oliverpeoples.com

Donate Used Eyeglasses:
www.lionsclubs.org/EN/content/vision_eyeglass_recycling.shtml

Drinking Glasses: "Smart Women Thirst for Knowledge"
www.uncommongoods.com/item/item.jsp?itemId=13037

Eighties sitcom character: Carol Seaver, *Growing Pains*
www.imdb.com/title/tt0088527

Euro Chanteuse: www.nanamouskouri.net

Eyeglass Cases: www.cinzia-designs.com

Insults: Coke-Bottles, Four-Eyes, Goggles, Mrs. Magoo

Librarian Action Figure:
www.mcphee.com/items/11247.html

Little Enid Coleslaw Doll:
www.presspop.com/en/shop/daniel_clowes/mini_enid_doll.html

Museum of Spectacles: www.brilmuseumamsterdam.nl

Prolific Author: Joyce Carol Oates
www.wiredforbooks.org/joycecaroloates/

Radio Show: www.freshair.com

Reading Glasses: www.amysacks.com

Song: "Yr Version of Cool" from *Music Makes Me Think of You*, Mad Planets,
www.taraemelye.com/songs/Yr_Version_Of_Cool.mp3

Sunglasses: www.eyesave.com

Superhero: Wonder Woman/Diana Prince
www.imdb.com/title/tt0074074/

T-shirt: "Reading Is Sexy"
www.buyolympia.com/9/Artist=Sarah+Utter

Television Show: www.gilmoregirls.com

Vintage Frames: www.fabulousfannys.com,
www.vintageiwear.com

Glasses Rule

These are just suggestions for choosing frames, of course. The GWG makes her own rules.

1. Make sure your eyes are centered in the lenses.
2. The experts recommend that frames be in proportion to your face size and in contrast to your face shape. You are also supposed to keep your eye, hair, and skin coloring in mind.

FACE SHAPE	FRAME	AVOID
heart	square oval	cat's-eye
oval	everything small	slender shapes
round	angular	round
square	soft round or oval	square
long	deeper than wide	small

Great Girl-with-Glasses Moments

1926: Dorothy Parker's couplet "News Item" published.

1938: First "bespectacled beauty contest" held in New York City by the Community Opticians Association to prove that "girls who wear glasses can be pretty lasses."

1964: *Harriet the Spy* published.

1965: British European Airways announces that for the first time it will be prepared to accept girls who wear glasses as air hostesses.

1969: Velma Dinkle proves herself only useful member of Scooby gang.

1971: Peppermint Patty's friend Marcie first mentioned by name in *Peanuts* comic strip.

1972: Shirley Chisholm announces her candidacy for president.

1976: Lina Wertmuller nominated for an Academy Award.

1980: Oscar winner Sophia Loren debuts her line of designer eyeglasses.

1982: Sarah Jessica Parker stars in *Square Pegs*.

1993: MTV VJ, snowboarder, and libertarian Kennedy is named Least Favorite VJ in *Rolling Stone*'s readers' poll.

1993: Janet Reno confirmed as Bill Clinton's attorney general.

1994: Ethan Hawke–directed video for Lisa Loeb's "Stay," from the *Reality Bites* soundtrack, premieres on MTV.

1994: David Letterman's mom, Dorothy, covers the Winter Olympics in Lillehammer, Norway, for *The Late Show*.

1997: Carrie Donovan appears in first of many Old Navy TV commercials.

1997: *Daria* premieres on MTV.

2000: Tina Fey debuts as coanchor on *Saturday Night Live*'s "Weekend Update."

2001: *Ghost World*, the movie based on Daniel Clowes's graphic novel, released.

2006: Frances McDormand, nominated for Best Supporting Actress, wears glasses to the Oscars.

2006: Janeane Garofalo dons her specs on the final episodes of *The West Wing*.

𝒫.𝒮.

Here's a reason not to get LASIK surgery. An ad for a New York clinic offering LASIK features a woman wearing a pair of those plastic New Year's Eve glasses. For the year 2002. The caption above her head reads WITH GLASSES I COULD NOT GET A DATE. The caption underneath her reads LASIK SOLVED THAT.

I never look back, dahling. It distracts from the now.
　　　　　　　　　　　—EDNA "E" MODE, *The Incredibles*

They Saw Light at the End of the Tunnel

Thank you to:

Emily Allison, Jennifer Anderson, Cara Bedick, Mika DeRoo, Denell Downum, Diana Finch, Jennie Guilfoyle, Holly Hartman, Jonathon Keats, Jason Logan, Michael Nagin, Margaret Kopp, Louise Quayle, Karen Sherman, Dutchy Smith, Helen Smith, Kara Spezeski, Joseph Walsh, Steven Walsh

and especially to:

Tricia Boczkowski
Carol Chinn
Elizabeth Kaplan

Matt Walker
Debbie Smith Walsh
Coley Walsh

and to all the Girls with Glasses.

Marissa Walsh is the coauthor of *Tipsy in Madras: A Complete Guide to '80s Preppy Drinking* and the editor of *Not Like I'm Jealous or Anything: The Jealousy Book*. In her early years she self-published a zine called *Indignant Gingham*. She lives in New York City.